ONE THING FOLLOWS ANOTHER

BEFORE YOU START TO READ THIS BOOK, take this moment to think about making a donation to punctum books, an independent non-profit press,

@ https://punctumbooks.com/support/

If you're reading the e-book, you can click on the image below to go directly to our donations site. Any amount, no matter the size, is appreciated and will help us to keep our ship of fools afloat. Contributions from dedicated readers will also help us to keep our commons open and to cultivate new work that can't find a welcoming port elsewhere. Our adventure is not possible without your support.

Vive la Open Access.

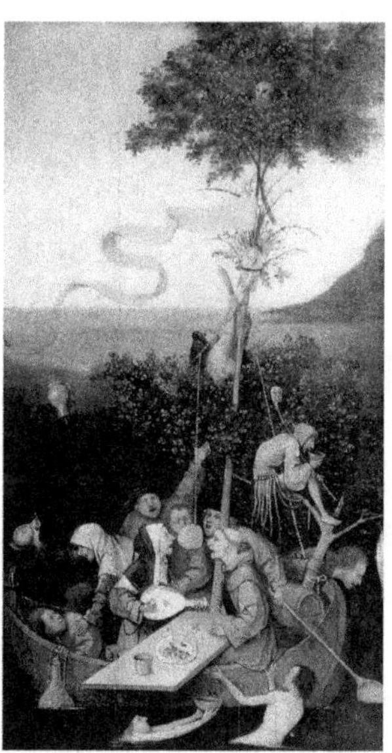

Fig. 1. Detail from Hieronymus Bosch, *Ship of Fools* (1490–1500)

First published in 2025 by punctum books, Earth, Milky Way.
https://punctumbooks.com

ISBN-13: 978-1-68571-188-7 (print)
ISBN-13: 978-1-68571-189-4 (ePDF)

DOI: 10.53288/0486.1.00

LCCN: 2025934121
Library of Congress Cataloging Data is available from the Library of Congress

Editing: SAJ and Eileen A. Fradenburg Joy
Book design: Hatim Eujayl and Vincent W.J. van Gerven Oei
Cover design: Vincent W.J. van Gerven Oei
Cover image: Jennifer Mack-Watkins

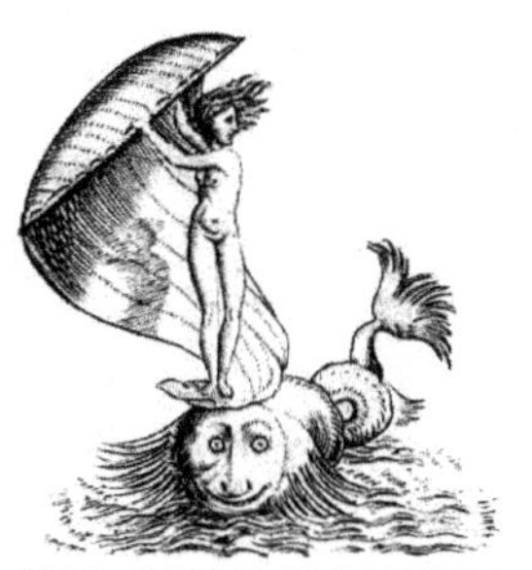

HIC SVNT MONSTRA

Sarah Rosenthal

Valerie Witte

One Thing Follows Another

Experiments in Dance, Art, and Life through the Lens of Simone Forti and Yvonne Rainer

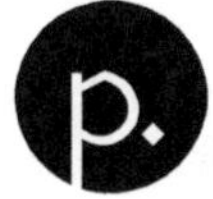

Contents

Acknowledgments

Our biggest debt of thanks goes to Simone Forti and Yvonne Rainer, whose choreography inspired this project as well as our earlier book *The Grass Is Greener When the Sun Is Yellow*, and who kindly made themselves available to us in numerous ways throughout the process. We are grateful for the opportunity to introduce new audiences to their radical ideas and practices. Our immersion in their work has enlarged our own poetics and taught us much about courage and artistic risk.

Thank you to punctum co-directors Eileen A. Fradenburg Joy and Vincent W.J. van Gerven Oei for taking on this book and marshaling it through the publication process. We cannot imagine a better home for this work. Thank you also to our peer reviewer, Erin Manning, who challenged us to take the experimental nature of this book even further through innovations in the book's organization. Gratitude to SAJ for taking such care in editing our manuscript, Hatim Eujayl for expertly laying out the book, and Livy Snyder for guiding us in promoting the work. Special thanks to Terry Morris for providing expertise on harm reduction. Much appreciation to Ralph Lemon for providing the Afterword — we have yet to see a more loving tribute to Yvonne and Simone. Deep appreciation to Jennifer Mack-Watkins for allowing us to reproduce the artwork that appears on the cover, and to the individuals who provided insightful and generous readings of the essays: Lucinda Childs, Serena Chopra, Yoshiko Chuma, Robert Glück, Daria Halprin, K.J. Holmes, Margaret Jenkins, Karla Kelsey, Alison Knowles, Petra Kuppers, Bebe Miller, Tracie Morris, Donna Uchizono, and Tyrone Williams. Thank you to Sally Silvers for her incredible generosity and support in helping this book prepare to launch. And thank you to rob mclennan, whose request for one thing (a blog post) led to another (this book).

FROM SARAH: Thank you to Valerie for being a stellar collaborator over many years of engaging with Rainer and Forti's work, first in our book *The Grass Is Greener When the Sun Is Yellow* and then with this essay collection. Your daring as an essayist sets a high bar, one that's been exciting to reach for. Your readiness to tackle tasks I find intimidating has both soothed and emboldened me. Your clear thinking, unswerving trustworthiness, and myriad skills have been indispensable to the fruition of both of our books. My gratitude to Mary Burger, Carrie Hunter, Dana Teen Lomax, and Denise Newman for their feedback on early drafts of essays. All my love to Steve Harris for his unflagging support.

FROM VALERIE: Thank you, Sarah, for your collaboration on this years-long project, including our previous book. Thank you for nudging me outside my comfort zone — encouraging me in exploring subject matter and form beyond what I knew I was capable of, and for nurturing this partnership so deeply, for so long. Thank you for keeping us on track and always driving us forward. Thank you for your friendship. Thank you to my friends Angela and Bill, who supported me in writing about them on a personal level in two of these essays. You have inspired me, and I am grateful to be able to share some of our experiences in these pages. Thank you, always, to Andrew.

Several of the essays in this collection were published in slightly different form in the publications that follow; our gratitude to the editors:

- "Animal Dance: Field Notes for Communicating Outside of Language" in *The Hunger*
- "Brutality of Borders: Experiments with Narrative or How One Things Follows Another" in *Cobra Milk*
- "Changing the Subject: Learning from Postmodernism's Focus on Context" in *Entropy*
- "Fire and Flood: Enacting Rehearsal as Performance" as a chapbook for above/ground press
- "The Five Positions: Assaying the Personal in Postmodern Art" in *Entropy*
- "Listening through the Body: An Exercise in Sustained Coordination" as a chapbook for above/ground press
- "Ordinary Movements: Erasing the Boundary between Performance and Reality" in *Storm Cellar*

The essay "How Will You Move: Including All of Us in the Dance" was a 2020 Gold Line Press chapbook finalist. A portion of the essay was selected as a semifinalist by the curators of the multidisciplinary art installation *home(Body)* and was published on the project's website. The essay also provided the voice-over language for Rosenthal's short film *We Agree on the Sun*, choreographed and performed by dancer-choreographer Ayana Yonesaka, and directed and edited by Jonah Belsky and Ames Tierney. The film has received numerous accolades including:

- Berlin Independent Film Festival — Winner, Best Experimental Short; selected for screening in online festival 2021
- Short. Sweet. Film Fest — Selected for screening in online festival 2021
- Toronto Independent Film Festival — Finalist
- Montreal Independent Film Festival — Finalist; selected for screening for the month of September 2020 on Toronto Film Channel
- NewFilmmakers New York — Semi-Finalist
- Southampton Film Week — Semi-Finalist; selected for screening in online festival 2020

To all artists whose creative risks offer new forms of being, knowing, and loving.

In memory of

Lyn Hejinian (5/17/1941–2/24/2024)
Tyrone Williams (2/24/1954–3/11/2024)
Steve Paxton (1/21/1939–2/20/2024)

Ordinary Movements: Erasing the Boundary between Performance and Reality

Valerie Witte

CHARACTERS

In order of appearance

SIMONE FORTI, a postmodern dancer–choreographer
SALLY BANES, an art and culture critic
JILL JOHNSTON, a dance and culture critic
MUSICIAN BOY, an artist and would-be lover
JOHN SHARP, a game designer and art historian
JULIA BRYAN-WILSON, an art critic and dance class participant
PIPPIN, the title character in *Pippin*
SCOTT MILLER, an author and founder of New Line Theatre
YVONNE RAINER, a postmodern dancer–choreographer
WENDY PERRON, a dancer–choreographer, teacher, and writer

ACT I

Growing up, my sister and I listened to the soundtrack of the musical *Pippin* (1972) so frequently, with such verve, that a permanent skip formed in the middle of "War Is a Science." (We eventually bought a replacement record.) I don't recall her ever expressing interest in any other musical, but she LOVED *Pippin*. She was a particular fan of Ben Vereen, who received a Tony Award for Best Actor for the role of Leading Player. One year she insisted we attend the annual Independence Day festival in downtown St. Louis just to see him onstage. To her chagrin, he performed only the approximately minute-and-a-half-long instrumental interlude from "Glory."

Since the 1960s, Simone Forti and Yvonne Rainer have been rebelling against the drama of modern dance, epitomized by the work of figures like

Martha Graham. Both artists rejected traditional narratives while incorporating everyday or task-based movements and game-based structures; further, Forti in particular eschewed the technically virtuosic choreography of figures such as Merce Cunningham. *SIMONE FORTI: "I remember watching my teachers, and feeling that I couldn't even perceive what they were doing, let alone do it. A teacher would demonstrate a movement, I'd see only this flashing blur of feet, and I wouldn't know what had happened. I just couldn't do it"* (Forti 1998, 34).

In third grade, when one of my paintings was selected for an art exhibit at the local mall, I named the piece "Morning Glow." This amused, or perhaps confused, my teacher. I later realized that Pippin sings this song after murdering his father. There are things we miss when we've never seen a show — even if we *have* memorized the soundtrack.

Equality was integral to the postmodern dance scene of the '60s, particularly in the work of the Judson Dance Theater, which Rainer co-founded. The emphasis on everyday movement, equal treatment of men and women performers, and at times, inclusion of both dancers and non-dancers, were all areas of focus for Rainer (Zdrojewski 2014, 42). *SALLY BANES: Judson's commitment to a process that de-emphasized formal technique and perfection in favor of freedom to explore through approaches such as improvisation and chance "was an aesthetic and even political choice, allowing for full participation by all the workshop members and giving the works an unpolished, spontaneous, 'natural' appearance." Anything — visual art, film, music — might be called a dance, as any actions of a dancer could be effectively "made strange" if framed as art* (Banes 1993, xviii).

I joined my Catholic school's church choir in fourth grade, a decision due more to the lack of other singing opportunities than any particular religious devotion. From fourth through seventh grades, I attended music class weekly, but the curriculum consisted primarily of our teacher playing '80s-era pop songs on the piano while we tried to "name that tune" (most memorably, "All I Want to Do Is Make Love to You," by Heart). I loved to sing — and I kept singing — eventually in my high school's choirs. Early sophomore year, I felt compelled to tiptoe outside my comfort zone and auditioned for my school's musical. Unfortunately, it was *Oliver!* Not the most exciting choice to my 15-year-old self, but I made the chorus, playing an orphan/"Fagin's boy." All girls (we were shorter than the students from the local all-boys schools who auditioned), we wrapped ace bandages around our chests and wore men's pajamas, using makeup to dirty our faces. (For a school seemingly terrified by the notion of gender nonconformity even today, the choice of this show and the approach to staging it now seem quite curious.) To my knowledge, everyone who'd auditioned made the cast. But still. I considered this an achievement, the director's frequent scoldings for my inability to produce a sufficiently evocative facial expression notwithstanding. Three years in the chorus — but I never considered auditioning elsewhere. Until senior year, when one of the boys' schools — which counts my dad and three brothers as alums — announced their next musical: the show whose songs I'd grown up singing in my basement for innumerable hours.

The idea that one needn't be technically trained as a dancer, singer, or artist to perform in such a realm, the erasure of boundaries between artists of various media. *JILL JOHNSTON: Artists danced, dancers played music, composers wrote poetry, poets made events. "Anyone can do it.... The idea hung porously in the atmosphere"* (Bennahum, Perron, and Robertson 2016, 134).

Around the time *Pippin* was announced as the spring musical, I began hanging out with some boys from the school, including a talented musician with whom I shared many mutual friends and acquaintances, as well as a birthday — a fact we discovered while waiting in line at a haunted house with our friends who had introduced us. I thought they were messing with us. (Lest the idea seem paranoid: One later flippantly wrote journal entries about our relationship — complete with our pasted-in school photos — as part of a semester-long English assignment that was eventually turned in to our teacher, Sister Kathryn. I was mortified.) *MUSICIAN BOY: You say it's your birthday ...*

Forti does not seem to have been deterred by her inability to perform complex dance steps requiring the "adult, isolated articulation" of choreographers like Cunningham. *SIMONE FORTI: "... the thing I had to offer was still very close to the holistic and generalized response of infants"* (Forti 1998, 34). Indeed this approach played out extensively in her *Dance Constructions* (1960–1961), a collection of pieces based on the idea of children's playground equipment that incorporated chance and ordinary movement. In these works, "dancers balanced on seesaws, embraced in a huddle of bodies, and stood still in hanging loops of rope." While abiding by "rules" set forth by Forti, the performers engaged in "pedestrian" gestures "lacking the arch stylization and technical finesse of traditional dance forms" (Lim 2016). This philosophy of movement subsequently found its way into much of Forti's oeuvre.

In a small theatrical production that fall, Musician Boy had a role in which he played guitar onstage. The carnation I gave him opening night rested on the music stand while he performed.

Some of Rainer's work also became associated with the idea of "pedestrian" actions or movements. The solo work *Ordinary Dance* (1962) featured Rainer's recitation of a monologue including the names of streets she'd lived on in San Francisco, accompanied by the repetition of simple movements; and in *We Shall Run* (1965), twelve performers ran continuously onstage in street clothes. These works seemed to reflect a shift from a perception of dance as a professional practice separate from everyday life to what she called "ordinary dance," reframing the form as a medium concerned with the natural movement of the body rather than the contrived movements of previous traditions (Sharp 2015).

Musician Boy was auditioning for *Pippin;* I decided to try out as well.

Rainer's *Trio A* (1966), which has in the past been performed by both dancers and non-dancers, arose from seeing, thinking, and moving in new ways. A less adorned style of performance, composed of a sequence of actions that draw on the movements the body makes in the process of everyday acts of work and play. *JULIA BRYAN-WILSON: Although* Trio A *is a highly technical dance that is difficult to perform, because of its task-based approach that draws from everyday, or found, movements, it is often characterized as made up of "pedestrian" movements. Many of the actions derive from ballet movements "made more ordinary, their dynamic range toned and tamped down, the flourishes and emphases taken out"* (Bryan-Wilson 2012, 61–62, 66).[1]

1 YVONNE RAINER: "pedestrian movements in most of Rainer's works" — MISTAKEN! NOT TRUE! And it is not true that there is less technique in *Trio A* than movement that requires training, which is one reason I stopped allowing it to be taught to untrained people —

AUTHORS: We refer to "pedestrian" movements several times throughout the manuscript, including to describe Rainer's work. Although she had extensive dance training — she studied ballet and trained with Martha Graham and Merce Cunningham — some of Rainer's early works incorporated everyday, or task-based movements, with a goal of creating the impression of "neutral doing"; as mentioned, *Ordinary Dance* (1962) involved the repetition of simple movements, and in *We Shall Run* (1965), participants jogged for several minutes onstage wearing street clothes. With these innovative, boundary-bending approaches, in the 1960s she — along with contempo-

Both Rainer and Forti took an interest in the work of Eadweard Muybridge, whose photography documents the dynamics of everyday, ordinary movement by both human and animal subjects (*The Heckscher Museum of Art* 2014). Muybridge served as an inspiration for Forti's piece *Huddle* (1961), which involves a group of performers situated in a huddle and, one by one, climbing over the mass of bodies in an improvisational manner. *FORTI: "'The performers are just doing what they need to do to climb or to sustain each other climbing'"* (Morse 2016, 125). The concept behind the piece is indicative of her desire to show an appreciation of "unadorned movement" in her work, "like the beauty of a plain wooden vessel" (Morse 2016, 125). For both Forti and Rainer, there was another reason for this preference for plain, unadorned movement. *FORTI: "'One aspect of modern dance I saw around me ... was a narcissism that didn't charm me a bit.... The interest in looking at movement, just plain generic movement, everyday movement, must partly have been a response to that narcissism'"* (Perron 2021).

ACT 2

Pippin is a study of the ordinary vs. the extraordinary — an examination of the value of living a regular life while being pulled toward something more meaningful. The title character, the son of Holy Roman Emperor Charles the Great (aka Charlemagne), sets out on a journey of self-discovery, expressing his need for the freedom to identify where he belongs in the world

---

raries including co-members of the Judson School — helped develop what became known as "ordinary dance" (Wood n.d.).

Over time, however, Rainer's work evolved away from including nondancers due to the physical and technical demands of the work; with this in mind, we have re-examined all instances of the word "pedestrian" and related terms such as "everyday" movements in the manuscript, and clarified our use of these terms to indicate the shift over time in Rainer's philosophy and approach.

Specifically regarding *Trio A:* This piece includes actions that draw on the movements the body makes in the process of everyday acts of work and play. While it was originally performed by both trained dancers and nondancers, it is indeed physically difficult to perform, according to critic Julia Bryan-Wilson, who learned the dance in a workshop at UC Irvine in 2008. It appears that this may have been one of the last times Rainer taught the dance, or allowed it to be taught, to nondancers. As Rainer notes in an interview published in *In Terms of Performance*, "*Trio A* is transmitted by five dancers authorized by me to teach it. I forbid *Trio A* to be learned from the video documentation of my own (flawed) execution of it from 1978. No one can teach or perform it without my permission" (Rainer 2016).

See the essay "Fire and Flood" in this collection for a bit more exploration of this form of transmission. The reasons that Rainer or any choreographer might choose to control a dance's transmission in our YouTube age are compelling and warrant further analysis. For the purposes of this book, we have made sure, thanks to Rainer's prompt, to clarify throughout that *Trio A* is no longer performed by nondancers.

in order to achieve his fullest potential. In "Corner of the Sky," Pippin wistfully sings of soaring like an eagle and rambling like a river, not satisfied with the idea of simply leading an uneventful, common life, settling for anything less than extraordinary. *PIPPIN: "I won't rest until I know I'll have it all"* (Schwartz 1972). In this introductory anthem, Pippin muses about destiny and dreams and how we cling to the comfort they promise.

For the singing tryout, I'd selected "Corner of the Sky" (I knew it by heart, of course). In the same all-girls audition group: a friend of mine who was more of a "drama kid" than I but not an extraordinary singer; and one of the best singers in our school, who afterward told me I'd done a good job. But the worrisome portion of the audition still lay ahead.

That idea of being special, made for greater things. In "Extraordinary," Pippin insists he deserves a chance to spread his wings, move beyond an ordinary existence, live a life of "superlatives." *PIPPIN: "When you're extraordinary / You gotta do extraordinary things"* (Schwartz 1972). But whether Pippin's journey is truly "extraordinary" — and whether striving for such a goal is a worthy endeavor — is questionable at best. *SCOTT MILLER: "We're watching someone who has all our faults and more, someone who is profoundly real and ordinary. We see ourselves in Pippin ... we do identify with him. We see in him our own desire to find perfection in our lives"* (Miller 1995).

Was my attempt to participate in this production an obviously misbegotten mission, initiated in a moment of bizarre, unfounded confidence, like when I ran for student council secretary in seventh grade? I'd been influenced by forces unusual for me — desire and fate. Wanting badly to be part of this particular show, to connect with this boy, led to the notion, a dream — perhaps tenuous — that I was meant to be in this cast.

Pippin's extreme normalcy is explicitly designed to create a connection with the audience; we are encouraged to identify with his inherently human feelings of insecurity, of seeking a place in which to belong — and thrive. The staging deliberately erases the boundaries between performance and reality, as characters interact with the audience, Leading Player inviting us, ultimately, to be complicit in Pippin's suicide (which doesn't come to pass) (Miller 1995).

Beginning as a child and then later throughout her career, Forti took a deep interest in studying the movement of animals, eventually working the task-oriented actions of these often-captive dancers into some of her works, perhaps most notably *Sleepwalkers* (1968), also known as Zoo Mantras. *WENDY PERRON: As a choreographer and dancer, by conferring such close attention on animals, she appeared to be "returning to the roots of movement"* (Perron 2021). Forti's consideration of animals was complex, as she felt a great deal of empathy toward them and, in many cases, focused on repetitive actions related to anxiety, which functioned as mechanisms for self-soothing (Bryan-Wilson 2015, 44). But at their most fundamental, these movements were unadorned, natural, and her animal-based works serve as another example of her privileging ordinary movement over elaborate or highly technical movements in her pieces.

Dance auditions for my school's musicals primarily involved a considerable number of jazz squares (whatever other choreographic elements long erased by my ignorance and the passage of time). This experience at the boys' school, by contrast, seemed to resemble an actual audition, featuring what I could only describe as "real dancing." The choreographer performed a series of steps that we were required to replicate. Her movements were a blur; I could scarcely identify what was happening or understand how the moves connected, one to the next, let alone physically perform them. Like hearing a series of phrases in an unfamiliar language and being expected to repeat them back fluently. I didn't believe performing in the singing chorus required stellar dance ability. As one of my brothers offered in a misinformed attempt to support me: *Pippin* doesn't have much dancing, right? (The musical was directed and choreographed by Bob Fosse, whose work included memorable dance numbers featuring moves that came to be recognized as his signature style.) Everyone else seemed fully capable of executing the steps while I floundered. I wished not for virtuosity but for the most basic, run-of-the-mill, unexceptional ability. (Everyone has their daydreams.) My drama friend laughed, not unkindly. As is my habit when faced with a challenge I deem unsurmountable, I shut down.

ACT 3

In the "Finale," as he nears the end of his journey, Pippin comes to accept that he is not extraordinary after all. Only when he embraces a so-called ordinary existence, appearing to settle down with Catherine, the one player who breaks protocol to save him from his supposed fate of death by suicide, does he achieve a level of maturity and a peace within himself. He discovers, ironically, that he will find freedom only once he stops seeking happiness in wild pursuits characterized by excess, drama, and glory. *PIPPIN: "I wanted magic shows and miracles / Mirages to touch ..."* (Schwartz 1972). Yet fulfillment isn't to be found through such grand exploits in far-off lands but rather at home, through living a simple, ordinary life.

MUSICIAN BOY: I'm so glad you didn't have to see me dance. Post-auditions, sheepish. (Little did he know ...)

JULIA BRYAN-WILSON: Trio A *heralded the arrival of an unprecedented vision for what dance could look like, the sorts of bodies allowed to participate in it. "It was claimed to be populist, egalitarian, and nonhierarchical, not only in its inclusion of non-dancers but also in its lack of a narrative, its evenness, and its lack of interest in classical emphasis, climax, and retreat"* (Bryan-Wilson 2012, 63). Rainer conducted a *Trio A* workshop at UC Irvine, in which Bryan-Wilson participated. How the juxtaposition of dancers and non-dancers — not isolated from each other but moving simultaneously in the same space — created interesting dynamics between them, opened new channels for engagement. *YVONNE RAINER: "[The non-dancers] knew what they could not do, like balance on one leg convincingly or roll the head around while doing a difficult side step. The [trained dancers] all had some dance training; they knew how to perform. What they didn't know and couldn't project was that sense of precariousness and achievement. My UCI 'amateurs' had weathered the fire of my obsessive attention, and it showed — in their pride, determination, and self-awareness"* (Bryan-Wilson 2012, 72).

MUSICIAN BOY: So ... I didn't see your name on the cast list. Later, a few days after the auditions. I tried to play it cool, no big deal. Tried not to think about months of practices, cast parties, hangouts missed. I don't remember if we talked much over the next few months. When the time came, seeing *Pippin* — a show I knew so well despite never having seen a performance — was bittersweet. There he was, playing "Simple Joys" onstage; there was my drama friend clearly having a blast in the singing chorus. (The "singing chorus" was aptly named — if there was any dancing involved, I didn't notice.) An article in the school's newspaper by a cast member and future bandmate of Musician Boy mentions the show's "platoon of 96 cast members" and quotes a freshman saying, "The cast is just perfect" (Laramie 1996).

At the end, when Catherine asks how he feels, Pippin's reply (the last line of the show) originally was "Trapped ... but happy." Fosse viewed this ending as too idealistic and insisted on striking the last two words. Later the show's writer, Stephen Schwartz, added them back (Miller 1995). The indecision around including these two words begs the question: Can Pippin — can any of us — genuinely come to accept, to embrace, the ordinary in our lives?

EPILOGUE

MUSICIAN BOY: So ... now that some time has passed .... Years later, after college, on the phone again. He wanted to talk about what had happened between us back then, when we "pseudo-dated." (A word he'd used to describe our relationship to our two friends, one of whom happened to have written the article about the "perfect" cast.) I wanted desperately to know what had, in fact, happened. At the same time, I wanted to extricate myself from this conversation as quickly as possible, given the high potential for embarrassment. I avoided the topic only to bring it up again in the following phone call. *MUSICIAN BOY: I admit, I had a bit of a crush on you ... but I wasn't head over heels or anything.* Sometimes an explanation is the most obvious, predictable, ordinary one. Sometimes an outcome is what we've expected all along. But we like "the way dreams have of sticking to the soul" (Schwartz 1972), so we allow ourselves to hope for a different result, the promise of something more exciting for ourselves, despite what our experiences and our stories about ourselves suggest.

Forti created art that mimicked the "generalized response of infants." Inspired by "natural" movements observed in children, on the playground, in the nursery school where she worked; in animals held captive at the Rome zoo. And from these subjects she developed pieces that challenged contemporary notions of what dance, or art, could be. Made us question what it means to be human or animal, free or confined. When limitation leads to innovation. (Sometimes constraints can be generative.) As Rainer, too, led explorations of the ordinary in dance, gestures often informed by everyday movements.[2] Inequities laid bare, then countered. A methodology culti-

2 YVONNE RAINER: I rarely use improvisation with regard to movement and never used chance procedures to create movement phrases — and after 1962 I stopped using chance procedures to sequence movement. Furthermore, I haven't taught *Trio A* to untrained people for the last 20 years!

AUTHORS: An earlier version of "Ordinary Movements" stated: "Rainer, too, led explorations of ordinary dance, movement defined not by technique but improvisation, chance." This has now been edited to more accurately reflect that improvisation and chance were among the techniques applied by members of the Judson Dance Theater in general.

We were both drawn to chance before we encountered Rainer and Forti's work and knew that we wanted it to be part of our own project. But, like Rainer and Forti, neither of us is or has ever been a strict follower of chance procedures in our work.

As discussed in the interstitial pieces that appear throughout this volume, Rainer has made clear from the beginning that she resists the notion

vated through rigorous artistic practice but also infused with the actions of daily life. Sometimes the ordinary can surpass the extraordinary — how both artists *have embraced,* have embodied this philosophy to varying extents in their bodies of work.

When I see Musician Boy now — at Powell's Books in Portland, at the Strange Folk Festival in St. Louis with our moms — what registers is not a sense of "what might have been" but the ways in which our relationship has been informed by an unusually high number of intersections. Not loss but an accumulation of — dare I say *fateful* — convergences. We still find it amusing that we were born the same day (though at different hospitals, we've confirmed), that his sister allegedly introduced mine to her husband, that our mothers attended the same physical therapy undergrad program, one year apart. There are other overlaps, I am sure, that I periodically forget and am reminded of when they arise in conversation. Extraordinary coincidence or ordinary happenstance: who's to say?

Maybe there *is* a kind of freedom in the ordinary — in lacking the highest level of aptitude, in resisting the desire to achieve perfection. In conducting research for this essay, I've uncovered a possible upside of being objectively ordinary, or even bad, at something. What we have to offer. *JULIA BRYAN-WILSON: "By the end of the run [of the UCI* Trio A *workshop] I was still the worst in the bunch, but I made a kind of peace with that, taking comfort in the notion that there is a generosity in being the worst"* (Bryan-Wilson 2012, 72). Words to live by, truly.

Notes

Italicized "dialogue" in the piece is composed of direct quotes or paraphrased ideas of the "characters."

It's notable that Vereen's character in *Pippin* leads the title character into wild pursuits characterized by excess, while Vereen himself has in recent years been accused of outrageous sexual misconduct. The ways in which his own story both chimes with and differs from that of his character deserves its own essay.

---

of chance dominating the compositional process. Speaking of a pivotal workshop she and Forti took with Dunn, she said, "[Chance] seemed to be the end-all. If you made it by chance, then anything was okay" (Morse 2016, 45). Forti, by contrast, continued to use chance and improvisation more liberally.

While Fosse is known for innovations such as jazz hands, turned-in knees, shuffling, and rolled shoulders, it is clear that many elements of his signature aesthetic are based on Black dance traditions. Rooted in African dance vernacular brought to America via the slave trade, early jazz dance — much like jazz music — laid the groundwork for trends that became extremely popular in twentieth-century America (*Gotta Dance: Fun. Fit. Focus.* 2021), eventually expanding into Broadway-style jazz and other related art forms. Fosse, among other white artists, gained fame through choreography undeniably informed by these earlier dance traditions (LaRoche 2020).

CORPUS LOCUS

In the 1950s, Yvonne Rainer, Simone Forti, and a handful of other young artists based in New York's Greenwich Village set out to challenge the practices and principles of professionalized dance. Inspired by the groundbreaking work of choreographers Anna Halprin, Robert Dunn, and Merce Cunningham, as well as composer John Cage, they were determined to change what dance was and could be.

Dance, as the most embodied form of creative expression, straddles nature and culture. Dance connects us to our wildness: we mince like egrets, prance like horses, hop like frogs. It belongs to all of us: from the time we can walk we can also twist and jiggle, in the kitchen or at a party or sitting in a traffic jam with our favorite tune cranked up loud. But dance — for better and worse — is also a force of enculturation. Professional dance encodes guidelines and narratives about proper conduct and appearance, not just onstage but in our lives. Ballet, the "high art" form that predominated in much of Europe and later in Russia and the US for several centuries, sent messages about gender roles: strong men carried weak, fluttery women. While the modernism of Martha Graham and Merce Cunningham opened up more empowering possibilities for women dancers, like ballet it requires submission to years of discipline and the execution of difficult and often contorted movements in order to enact value-laden ideas about art and beauty. Even burlesque, often framed as "low art," requires exaggerated poses and gestures meant to signal the dancer's sexual appeal — traditionally, the female dancer's appeal for men, though the form has recently been queered in compelling ways.

Rainer and Forti, along with their peers, took on and shook up these expectations. They replaced the stylized motions and costumes of ballet and modern dance with androgynous, comfortably dressed bodies moving in fluid and undramatic ways. Rainer featured trained (and for a time, untrained) dancers collaborating on ordinary tasks while Forti developed a style of movement informed by the instinctive, repetitive movements of children and zoo animals, and also often featured collaboration and untrained dancers in her work. With their peers and their mentor Halprin, they moved performance out of conventional venues and into public zones including the street, the plaza, and the warehouse loft.

The group was unique in that it comprised professionally trained dancers, others who had tried and failed to meet the austere standards of professional dance, and artists from other disciplines, like sculptors and painters. It also included several women at a time when men still dominated art forms other than dance. Since dance had always featured women, and women such as Halprin and Graham had paved the way, it makes sense that serious female innovators of the time found a home base there.

From Virtuosity to Possibility: Dreaming a Poetics of Liberation

Sarah Rosenthal

The introduction to *Radical Bodies: Anna Halprin, Simone Forti, and Yvonne Rainer in California and New York, 1955–1972* refers to the "feminist eradication of virtuosity" in the work of these three artists (Bennahum et al. 2016, 22). It's not hard to see why eradicating virtuosity can be understood as a worthy feminist project — doing so creates a level playing field. If virtuosity is devalued, then the emerging artist need not be diminished, or outright erased, by the canon of white male virtuosos in every art form, along with the trappings and trainings that prop them up. If virtuosity is devalued, an artist might assert that dances designed to be inclusive, featuring many kinds of bodies, capacities, or types of movement, are as worthy exemplars of art as dances based on traditional training with its prohibitions and selectivity. If virtuosity is devalued, the specific forms of virtuosity found in both traditional ballet and burlesque, which allow female ambition yet configure the female body in its dainty or bawdy costume as eye candy to be consumed by the male gaze, enacting a narrative of conquest by the male, are no longer relevant. A space is opened up for the woman to inhabit her skin, stand her ground, move across it as she will — as she wills. She can refigure not only the meaning of the dancer's body but also the dynamics between dancer and spectator. Because if dance is no longer predicated on woman as delectable morsel serving the pleasure of the male (audience) member, then both the dancer's and the spectator's roles can change, in ways to be determined through active investigation.

And whatever terms we use, Rainer and Forti's work opened up dance in all of these ways. But both artists take issue with the phrase "feminist eradication of virtuosity," albeit for different reasons. Let's start with the term "feminist." Wendy Perron reports on a panel discussion she moderated at the University of California, Santa Barbara "Radical Bodies" symposium in January 2017:

> When I asked each of them if they felt they were pre-feminist (since feminism didn't surge until the 1970s), Yvonne allowed as how she and Simone had, over the years, an ongoing argument about this. Yvonne said she embraced feminism but didn't feel she had the right to call herself that because she wasn't an activist. Simone, on the other hand, said she did not feel drawn to feminism. Her father had told her she

> could be whatever she wanted, and her first husband, minimalist sculptor Robert Morris, had encouraged her and helped her become an artist. (Perron 2017)

I invited Rainer and Forti to read an earlier version of this essay. Rainer clarified her position: "If I said at some point in the '60s that I was not a feminist, I am sure I qualified such a statement with the fact that I did not consider myself an activist so did not think I deserved such an identity — but that stance was very short-lived, more so than some feminists have suggested — by the late '60s I considered myself an avowed feminist" (Rainer 2021). Forti expanded on her statement to Perron, making it clear that her resistance to the term goes well beyond the question of whether it applies to her personally: "I'm sure that a lot of good has come through feminism. I also feel that as a way of seeing the world feminism is brutally limiting and destructive to our ability to see people, women and men, as they are" (Forti 2019). Turning to the words "eradication of virtuosity," Forti did not take issue with that language, but Rainer (again in response to the earlier version of this essay) wrote: "'Redefined virtuosity' is more apt, and for me had nothing to do with feminism!" (Rainer 2021).[1]

As much as I'm excited by the radical concept of eradicating virtuosity, and much as I can point to the fact that Rainer herself wrote the phrase "No to virtuosity" early in her career, I can see that it is an extreme statement, and I can appreciate Rainer's subsequent move away from it (2008). It's arguable that at least some form of virtuosity is part and parcel of any

1 AUTHORS: The version of the essay that Rainer commented on grounded itself in a statement she made early in her career that rejected virtuosity outright and took several other strong positions — words that to this day dance critics and aficionados refer to. Rainer's pithy comment regarding the essay's premise helped us recognize more fully what it means to be an artist who wants and needs to morph their thinking over time, and the frustration of continuing to have one's work viewed via positions taken early in one's career. As a result, the entire essay has been revised to more carefully reflect Rainer's evolving aesthetic and to directly address Rainer's shift from a rejection of virtuosity to a redefinition of it.

Similarly, it was valuable to learn that Rainer does not see her relationships to virtuosity and to feminism as connected. Forti, who also read the earlier version of the essay, raised her own strong objection about the piece's discussion of feminism in her and Rainer's work. The revised essay addresses both artists' comments directly, leading to what we believe is a more accurate and nuanced discussion.

As a result of Rainer's comment, the essay "Ordinary Movements" has also been revised. The version Rainer read stated that she and Forti both largely rejected virtuosity in favor of everyday task-based movement. This was true more so in the case of Forti, who quickly realized she was unable to perform complex choreography à la Merce Cunningham, whereas Rainer had several years of formal dance training.

See our responses to Rainer's comment in "How Will You Move: Including All of Us in the Dance," n. 2, for more on how we revised this collection to better reflect her evolving aesthetic.

serious art-making practice. In service to a more nuanced, realistic framing of their contribution and out of respect for these artists' own way of framing their work, I am hereby discarding the black-and-white term "eradication" in favor of Rainer's "redefinition" and similar, less absolutist terms. Certainly it's safe to say both Forti and Rainer's work has *redefined* virtuosity throughout their long careers, such as Forti's projects inspired by animal movements and her *Dance Constructions*, in which performers improvise pedestrian movements based on rules provided by Forti, and Rainer's many versions of *Trio A*, in which performers — originally a mix of dancers and non-dancers — wear street clothes and make identical movements together but not in unison, and never make eye contact with the audience.

So that leaves the term "feminist." Note that while Perron carefully distinguishes between pre-feminism and feminism, neither Rainer nor Forti splits hairs on this, and neither will I. Reflecting on Forti's position, I can see that applying that term to her and Rainer's work could be understood as limiting. I hate to put the words "feminism" and "limiting" next to each other, even for a moment, because for me there is never anything limiting about feminism. The title and message of bell hooks's book *Feminism Is for Everybody* resonates with me. Sexism hurts us all. Until we've completely uprooted it — and when will that be? — I believe we need feminism. But it's also true that in the '60s and '70s Rainer and Forti were involved with several converging movements and lines of thinking that did not have to do with feminism per se, but that all challenged the concept of virtuosity.

Judson Dance Theater, of which Rainer was a founding member, was formed by a group of individuals who had taken a choreography workshop with Robert Dunn, a composer and accompanist to choreographer Merce Cunningham. (Forti took Dunn's class too but did not join Judson.) Via Cunningham and composer John Cage, Dunn had become enamored with the use of chance procedures to create art. Just as Cage, deeply influenced by both Zen Buddhism and Dada — in particular the work of Marcel Duchamp — combined chance with a radically inclusive concept of what sorts of sounds might constitute music, so Dunn encouraged his students to create dances using chance combined with everyday and task-like gestures, from eating to talking to running to climbing. This workshop, as well as the Judson Dance Theater group formed by Rainer and other students of Dunn, included non-dancers such as Robert Rauschenberg, Robert Morris, and Carolee Schneemann. According to Carrie Lambert-Beatty (2008, 42), "While Judson dance often included passages of modern or balletic technique [...] one of the group's lasting contributions was to put the line between dance and ordinary behavior under erasure."

Anna Halprin, a choreographer based in Marin County, also had a significant impact on Judson Dance Theater and Forti. Forti studied extensively with Halprin before moving to New York, and later Rainer and Trisha Brown also attended Halprin's workshop. Halprin's groundbreaking work in the areas of improvisation, speaking while dancing, the use of natural and public settings for dances, and the building of dances around tasks and scores all contributed to the evolving vocabulary of Forti, Rainer, and their peers, even as the latter approaches were used by Cage and Dunn as well. The fact that Dunn, Cage, and Cunningham have tended to receive most of the credit, even from Rainer herself, for introducing tasks and scores until the 2017 publication of *Radical Bodies* can be seen as its own feminist issue.

Contemporary movements with which Rainer and Forti had varying degrees of involvement included Fluxus and Happenings, both of which also challenged the traditional notion of virtuosity. A typical Fluxus event was scored as a short set of instructions that could be performed by anyone at any time, dissolving all difference between performer and audience. In addition, Fluxus events often explicitly included performative roles for spectators. Ken Friedman's *Cardmusic for Audience* involved audience members each picking a number and creating a sound and gesture that could be performed from their seats. A conductor pointed one at a time to onstage performers who, when cued, showed numbered cards prompting particular audience members' sounds and gestures (Lambert-Beatty 2008, 30). Happenings were similarly designed to break down the distance between performer and spectator. As Allan Kaprow (1993, 15–16), inventor of the term *Happening*, said:

> You come in as a spectator, and maybe discover that you're caught in it after all [....] [There are] long silences when nothing happens, and you're sore because you've paid $1.50 contribution, when bang! there you are facing yourself in a mirror jammed at you. [...] You giggle because you're afraid, suffer claustrophobia, talk to someone nonchalantly, but all the time you're *there*, getting into the act.

As a group, Rainer, Forti, and the artists and theorists with whom they were in contact broke down boundaries between art forms — socially by making art and discussing ideas together and forming friendships and sometimes romances with one another, and conceptually by seeing themselves as artists first and as dancers, choreographers, sculptors, painters, writers, and so on second. They were asking fundamental questions about what art was and did. The influences flowed freely in various directions. For example, Morris and Richard Serra were both deeply impacted by Rainer's early ideas — which she has said were influenced by Pop Art, Duchamp, and Dada, along with comedic work by W.C. Fields, Charlie Chaplin, and Buster Keaton — about the relationship of the art object to space and to audience (Bennahum et al. 2016, 124). And each artist filtered the ideas and processes they were learning from one another as needed. For example, Rainer early on discarded Cage, Cunningham, and Dunn's adherence to chance operations and has never favored the intermingling of performers and audience members during performances, unlike artists involved in Fluxus and Happenings.

In light of all these multidirectional influences and themes, is it appropriate to describe Rainer and Forti's work as feminist? Should we adopt the view that feminism is at most one among many elements that frame their work? Or can everything they did and thought be subsumed under the feminist umbrella?

As deeply as I respect Rainer and Forti's right to choose their own terms for their identities and their art, like the authors of the introduction to *Radical Bodies,* I do see the work of both (as well as the work of Halprin) as feminist. I don't think it's accidental that these women who first started making art in the '50s played a significant role in challenging a status quo in which virtuosity and male dominance of the art world were inseparable.* They made dances that include dancers doing non-dancerly actions in non-dancerly attire; their dances feature men and women moving in non-gendered ways, defy traditional narrative arcs of quest and conquest, and challenge the idea of the dancer, especially the female dancer, as eye candy. If those things don't add up to a feminist vision, I don't know what does. And part of my definition of what makes something feminist is its effect on me as a woman. Rainer and Forti's challenge to virtuosity carves out more space for me to move in.

Is it only now that it does so, after I've inhabited the planet for six decades and made art for half of that period? Or did their vibrant presence in the avant-garde New York art world in the late '60s and early '70s somehow waft across to my Chicago childhood and impact my relationship to movement at that time?

In 1970, when I was in fifth grade, I started folk dancing. It was something a wide network of kids from Hyde Park on Chicago's South Side had gotten into. The origin of this phenomenon may have been Circle Pines, a leftie summer camp attended mostly by Hyde Parkers, which offered folk dancing among its activities. I knew a lot of Circle Pines kids, so I guess one of them invited me along to the weekly Wednesday folk dance evening at the University of Chicago's International House. A lot of the kids spent most of the evening chatting and flirting in chairs that lined the walls of the enormous auditorium. I remember sitting with a girl a couple years older than me, who described in vivid detail getting a back massage from a boy she liked. At some point, he asked her to turn over and massaged her chest. She was all honey and flames telling me this. Stunned by a combination of envy and revulsion, what could I do? Leave her side. Get up and dance.

My home was an unhealthy place to come of age as a girl, given my father's combination of lewd and dominating behavior and my mother's tolerance of it. The bad training I received at home made me a magnet for sexist treatment by men in the culture at large. But when I left the hothouse of the adolescent sidelines and joined the dance, I had a way to be in my body that felt safe, competent, pleasurable — the opposite of how I had felt since the moment I'd felt the first hormonal stirrings.

Folkdance is the original dance, the dance of humans in community, the body's conversation with spirit. There are at times virtuosic displays of strength and agility, but the audience for such feats is not seated silently, hands in laps. They're standing in a circle around the virtuoso, whistling and clapping, egging the person on to go higher, faster, wilder — and then it's someone else's turn. The more hungry you are to learn, the more time you spend hovering and stumbling behind others as their bodies show you the way. You learn to latch onto the music and let it do the heavy lifting, moving you in the rhythm of its particular culture. But as much as strivers, myself included, will always strive, the bottom line is acceptance. Any body, graceful or clunky, can show up and dance.

It was a world. The adults were hippy intellectuals, the lion's share of them connected to the university. They were busy with their own socializing and flirting, all of which was analyzed closely by us kids, or at least by me. At the same time, they accepted us, enjoyed us, and taught and learned from us.

It was a world that shared certain tenets with Rainer and Forti's world. At the very least, in the eyes of mainstream America, the progressives who gathered each Wednesday night to study, honor, and preserve centuries-old folk dances from every continent would have been relatively indistinguishable from these Greenwich Village avant-garde artists, who over time got teaching and performing gigs at universities around the country where cutting-edge ideas were welcome. Once in that room together, at least some of the folk dancers would have appreciated or even jumped in and participated in Rainer's *Continuous Project — Altered Daily*, with Rainer teaching them dances within the performance context. Nor is it hard to picture Rainer, Forti, and their colleagues spending an evening learning traditional dances, eager to absorb what they could to feed their own projects. Both groups would have recognized their shared embrace of a virtuosity that is compatible with inclusion.

Because every dance could be performed at any level, from nimble stepping to clumsy shuffling, it was a particularly inviting form for a tormented pre-teen who yearned to participate in beauty. One of my favorites was sandansko oro. In a workshop put on by visiting instructors from Macedonia, I learned every nuance of the swinging, syncopated dance. Once you felt confident in the steps of a line dance, you could take the lead, and I always rushed to do so. I danced with the fullest gestures possible. Just as the music poured through the room and out the windows and doorways, to be caught by the ears of students crossing the campus, I wanted the pure joy, our motion ancient yet alive, crafted yet liberated, earthy yet effervescent, to spill into the world, up into the sky. I wanted the perfectly coordinated, buoyant swing of my arm to enter the arm of the person next to me, and through that person's body to the next, as the infectious music drew more and more bystanders into the lengthening line. I needed to dance so vigorously that by the time the music stopped, I was willing — even glad — to flop panting onto a chair for a moment — only to be yanked into the next dance by the familiar opening bars of another beloved number. I needed to dance with such abandon that I could make it through another week of debilitating insecurity and paranoia on every other front — home, school, and social life.

A couple nights ago, after days of puzzling how to execute the assignment of this essay — to bring into relation with one another the chance-and-dance-generated topics of "feminist eradication of virtuosity" and my history with this particular folk dance — I dreamed:

> I'm at the folk dance gym, wanting to lead sandansko oro. I'm ready to cover ground, gesture large. Will I knock people over and be shamed? My old friend X, who also has a history with folk dance, as well as with ballet, enters. Her rigidity and emotional repression are painfully obvious. A sweet, hippy idealistic man she's in love with, her visual twin — same straight chestnut hair, same tall, lanky build — has gently pulled away, turned off by her inability to connect. I try to help her thaw through a guided process, but she rejects my efforts. When I apologize, she brushes off even that. Anything's too much contact. She takes me outside and shows me a hive of small snow cubbies; shelved in each is a sleeping rabbit — long, muscular, a bit bloody, like unskinned meat in a freezer. She expertly answers my question: do they ever wake during hibernation? Yes, briefly sometimes they do. She has so much affection for these animals in their dead sleep.

The dream obligingly dives right into the assignment. It foregrounds a classically feminist issue: how does a woman take up space, do her dance, express herself as fully as possible without knocking over others and being shamed for stepping out of line? That is the question posed by the dreaming "I," a part of this dream consciousness that has tasted freedom and wants more. The friend — another part of this consciousness — enters at the tail end of this question, without missing a beat. This part is still as repressed as the fifth grader I was for most of the hours outside of each Wednesday evening, as repressed and resigned — let's make a large gesture here — as many grown women still are. (Tarana Burke coined the phrase *Me Too* in 2006, yet it took the 2017 revelations about Harvey Weinstein's horrific behavior to kick the #MeToo movement into high gear.) Even this part longs for connection with the other — in the dream, a beautiful male counterpart — but is incapable of a vibrant, sexual, passionate love. Instead, this part can only connect with our robust, muscular, leaping animal nature if it is safely out of commission, frozen in a deathlike sleep. Yet hibernation holds the promise of spring, of thaw, however much the state of these creatures slotted into their morgue-like snow shelves might fill our field of vision. These creatures will bound again; the dream "I" will dance sandansko oro full-out, fearless, exuberant — this communal dance that all are welcome to join.

Rainer, Forti, and others in their circle such as Brown, Schneemann, and Lucinda Childs did so much to carve out space for others, artists or not, who came after them. It's important to note that this was a very white crowd. Anna Halprin began to address race head-on in her work in the '60s; others, notably Rainer, have done so more recently (Kale 2015 and Fischer 2018). To varying degrees, these white women replicated the exclusion of people of color in the same way men have excluded women (Perron 2017). Still, through their challenge to the status quo, they helped open doors that others have been able to dance through.

Yet their path was, and is, not easy. Forti's art took backstage to that of husband Robert Whitman for a number of years. While she chose this freely, it may have led to the under-recognition of her work over many years. It took Rainer decades to come out as queer. Both were key in developing Minimalism, and key Minimalist men such as Morris and Serra openly acknowledge and celebrate their influence — but look up the movement online to see long lists of dudes with maybe Agnes Martin thrown in. We're all still up against entrenched power structures; we all have more waking up to do, more asserting of our right to leap. The dream can be read as acknowledging this ongoing struggle.

That's a lot to siphon off from the fount of the unconscious — but wait, there's more. Last night I dreamed:

> I'm Yvonne Rainer. Simone Forti and I learn each other's dances, performing them for one another. She moves laterally, mime-like, as if behind a sheet of glass. She has put on white pancake makeup, red lipstick, and a rakish hat — abstract clown suit — in order to inhabit my persona. I didn't do anything comparable to my appearance, but in executing her dance I move laterally as well, facing her as if behind my own floor-to-ceiling invisible barrier.

I am struck by the emphatic "yes" and the intriguing "no" of this dream. It tells me how deeply touched I am by Rainer and Forti: I know their work (especially Rainer's, which I've studied more) well enough to dream an obvious reference to Rainer's 1962 dance *Satie for Two*, in which Rainer and Trisha Brown wore clownlike costumes and, in a photo I've seen, appear to move as if pressed between flat surfaces. But beyond that, it tells me that I know what I might call my "inner Rainer" — the artist who converses through her medium, who mirrors what she perceives, who both teaches and learns. And I know the Forti in me, although she's other than the dream "I" — maybe, as noted, because I haven't studied her as much.

The costume Forti dons in order to accurately represent the "Rainer me" may point to the role of both intellect and humor in Rainer's and my work, and it invites comparison of Forti and Rainer's art, as well as reflection on the nature of persona in performance. Dream-Forti feels the need to costume herself to perform dream-Rainer's work, while dream-Rainer does not feel called to mask herself in order to perform dream-Forti's work. One reading of this is that it reflects the nature of each artist's aesthetic; while both are intellectual powerhouses, Rainer leads with her mind a lot, whereas Forti has done a lot of work to get as close as possible to animal movement, animal instinct — so Forti needs to alter herself, add a layer, to inhabit Rainer's creativity, but Rainer needs no props to inhabit that of Forti. Another reading allows us to think about the dialectics of attempting to strip away anything that covers the truth we try to get at as artists. It's possible to strip a lot away, as described above. At the same time, the dream argues, persona is a fundamental element of art. To wit: in this dream I inhabit the persona of Rainer, just as Forti makes obvious her inhabitation of Rainer's/my persona.

Like Frida Kahlo's painting *The Two Fridas*, this dream offers up a deeply feminist image — two aspects of a female consciousness in communion. Yet the two Fridas, for all their obvious signs of merging, maintain separate selves — indicated by their very different costumes and by the fact that they gaze, not at one another but out at the viewer. So too do this dream-Rainer and dream-Forti both merge and remain separate, each enacting the mime of moving behind a sheet of glass. We're not all one — Rainer and Forti remain separate — and I'm not either of them, even if my dream allows me to get deliciously close to and even embody my ideas about these inspiring, and yes, in my view, *feminist* icons, based on my research on their works and lives. We each maintain our individual visions even as we dialogue with those of others. That is a "no" that is also a "yes" — a yes to possibility.**

Notes

* I'm not suggesting that Rainer, Forti, and their colleagues were the first to push their way into a male-dominated art space. Women have been finding ways to do that for millennia. But the period in which Rainer and Forti began working was one in which male domination of the art world and the concept of the virtuoso artist were so tightly intertwined that these women's challenge to virtuosity (a challenge some men also took on) was innovative, courageous, and, from a feminist point of view, necessary.

** I am indebted to Michael Palmer for the idea of a "no" that is also a "yes"; see my interview with him in Palmer (2010, 195). Coincidentally, Palmer has been deeply involved with postmodern dance through his decades-long collaboration with choreographer Margaret Jenkins.

A/POLITICAL ARTISTS

Rainer, Forti, and their peers did not initially identify their work as political. Yet over time, various members of their circle tackled political issues explicitly or implicitly. Halprin addressed race directly in her work beginning in the late 1960s. Rainer, who came out as queer in middle age, has over time taken on issues of gender, global politics, and race. Forti's work can be seen as environmentalist. And in retrospect the work seems protofeminist — though it must be acknowledged that the artists themselves have complicated relationships (and in the case of Forti, flat-out resistance) to this term. Several of these artists, still working, embody anti-ageism at its most empowering: they perform and teach, listen and learn, befriend and collaborate with people young enough to be their grandchildren.

In any case, all the work generated by this group is implicitly political in that, from the beginning, it has defied dehumanization and commodification. While most of us are free to move our bodies in ways we choose — sip a glass of water, sprawl on a couch, burst into a run — at the same time, our physical movements are controlled through messages we receive from the larger culture and its institutions. We are encouraged, ordered, or forced to move in certain ways and have certain physical experiences. Bodies raise hands in salute or for permission, line up, suck in stomachs, smile brightly, teeter on heels, and repeat speedy motions to the point of disability. Bodies have guns pointed at them. Bodies are penetrated violently. Bodies pace in cages. Bodies are hung. And the power structure, including political, economic, and cultural interests, reserves its most directed efforts to constrict the behaviors of bodies it has deemed Other. In our own era, the threats, abuse, and murder perpetrated by that power structure against members of marginalized groups have been met with fierce resistance by the Black Lives Matter and #MeToo movements, shining an especially bright light on the issue of corporeal freedom versus control.

Rainer and Forti's work holds up a loving mirror that invites us to inhabit our bodies and daily lives fully, and find out what we can learn from this acceptance and acute attention. It models ways to tackle tough issues while making room for joy, play, and humor. Metaphorically, it invites us all to the dance, just as we are, judgments checked at the door. We have always needed this, and we need it now.

Performance at Play: The Art of Exploring Natural Movement

Valerie Witte

|| *Plié, pas de bourrée* only sounds. uttered
over enacted

continuous *body*
At the
playground
You'd jump swing

vault
forward to cherry drop
across fields
I'd come
an array of leotards
hanging

Sometimes we played

I'd push
buttons leaping to
hurl fireballs.
"This is boring," "Let's do

splits

Slap hips like a
drum. The way your body.

effortless

play. ||

|| *Plié, pas de bourrée, tour jeté.* I knew only sounds.

The language
of dance *A*
continuous bending *outward, upper body*
held upright. || At the
playground three bars
You'd hoist your legs over, swing
Until, eventually,
vaulting
forward to land. A cherry drop, I came to learn.
across the baseball fields

leotards
from the cabinets. Your mother sewing
Sometimes we played
Super Mario
I'd
leap to
punch bricks hurl fireballs. Only
virtually could I "This is boring," you'd say. "Let's do

splits, in the middle Or another,
more peculiar maneuver

The way you could contort your body.
inconceivable
appeared effortless, solely to entertain yourself and
whomever else you
sure knew how to play. ||

|| *Plié, pas de bourrée, tour jeté.* I knew only the sounds. Words uttered over and over, as you enacted the movements. From the age of three, enrolled in tap, jazz, ballet — three, four days a week. The language of dance flitting in the air around you. Heels firmly to the floor. *A* smooth and continuous bending of the knees *outward, upper body held upright.* || You seemed always to be in motion. || At the school playground three parallel bars of varying heights situated beside each other. You'd jump to grab one, hoist your legs over, swing back and forth upside-down, building speed, momentum. Until, eventually, when high enough, releasing your legs, arms outreached, vaulting yourself forward to land. A cherry drop, I came to learn. And witness countless times. || You lived immediately across the baseball fields and I'd come over at least once a week. We spent hours in your kitchen, an endless array of leotards, dresses, jackets, skirts in various stages of progress hanging from the cabinets. Your mother always sewing something for one of your many recitals. || Sometimes we played Super Mario Bros. on your badly worn Nintendo system. (I blew into the cartridge on a regular basis to help it along.) I'd push those black arrows and red buttons repeatedly, indefinitely — leaping to collect coins, punch bricks, jumping on enemies, hurling fireballs. Only virtually could I move like this. "This is boring," you'd say. "Let's do something else." You tired of such sedentary pastimes quickly. || Soon after you'd be in splits, in the middle of conversation. Or another, more peculiar maneuver — lying on your back, legs wrapped around you, ankles secured behind your neck. Slap your face-up hips like a drum. The way you could contort your body. A position impossible for most, inconceivable both for its absurdity and the flexibility required. For you, appeared effortless, executed solely to entertain yourself and whomever else happened to be in the room. || Like no one else, you sure knew how to play. ||

The embrace of "natural" movement, and the related concept of kinesthetic awareness, were central to the approaches of Simone Forti and her mentor and teacher Anna Halprin, both of whose work extended the philosophy of Halprin's teacher Margaret H'Doubler. H'Doubler, who founded the first dance program at an American university, viewed dance as both an art and a science, and she taught dance based on the idea of natural body movement — that is, movement that did not require formal technique. To H'Doubler, "'faulty, habitual movement' could be banished by reeducating the body toward natural movement." She used the term "kinesthetic sense" to describe the ability to develop a sense of awareness of even the slightest bodily changes brought about by movement (Morse 2016, 19–20).

Halprin was greatly influenced by H'Doubler's approach. She noted:

> As we discover how to move naturally, operating out of universal principles that govern all bodies, we will gradually replace old tired habits with rhythmic and relaxed movement. [...] I believe natural movement has many values for you: you can be yourself and discover your own style rather than being like someone else or taking on an imposed style. (Morse 2016, 15)

The possibility of being allowed — encouraged even — to develop a style completely one's own, unencumbered by formal dance requirements, carries with it a powerful sense of freedom, suggesting that one need not possess the specific skill and training typically associated with dance to enjoy, and excel at, the art form. This embrace of natural movement and kinesthetic awareness was also deeply resonant for Forti, who believed "the natural was transparent and immediate — and a way of moving that was so thoroughly practiced it had become naturalized" (Morse 2016, 19–20). Forti's emphasis on natural movement is perhaps why she describes herself as a movement artist rather than a dancer or performance artist.

Moreover, these approaches emphasized play as a way to achieve this desired natural state. Halprin believed that children's play activity derived from innate responses and behaviors unaffected by convention or expectation; children "emblematized the desired 'natural,' presenting a model that adults, alienated from their physicality and their real selves, might emulate" (Morse 2016, 21). Children's play was also an early source of material for Forti, particularly in her *Dance Constructions.* These pieces are, in a sense, games for adults built on the idea of children's playground equipment. In *See-Saw* (1960), performers balance on opposite ends of a seesaw while periodically reading aloud from a magazine or improvising other vocalizations. *Rollers* (1960) features two performers sitting in a wooden box with wheels, ropes attached, while performers or audience members swing them throughout the performance space. In *Hangers* and *Accompaniment for La Monte's "2 sounds"* (1961), a performer stands, swaying, on a rope loop, like a swing. *Huddle* (1961), in which a mass of performers spontaneously climb over one another, one by one, until arriving at the other side of the formation, resembles a football-style huddle or a children's play structure (Morse 2016, 23). And *Slant Board* (1961) involves three or four performers using ropes to move around a wooden ramp leaning at a 45-degree angle against a wall. The piece echoes Halprin's interest in gravity and task-based movement while also creating "a playground for the adult body that defamiliarizes a common experience such as walking uphill and asking viewers and participants to rethink the forces at play on the body in physical space" (Kelsey 2017).

Forti came up with the ideas for these sorts of structures by observing children at play in multiple settings, first through her work as a dance teacher at an all-girls school in San Rafael, CA and then through work at a nursery school in New York. The use of equipment similar to what would be present in a playground offered formal limits and structure, as well as a way to eliminate the adult body's ingrained physical habits, a goal she shared with Halprin (Morse 2016, 23). Furthermore, this approach dovetailed with Forti's physical abilities and movement style; as she herself admitted, she was unable to execute complex choreography, choosing instead to create and perform work that mimicked the "generalized response of infants" (Forti 1998, 34).

Outside of these specific playground equipment-based structures, her observations of children as well as what she gleaned from training with choreographer Robert Dunn further deepened her sense that dance could encapsulate play, among other things. Here she connects her experience with a child from the nursery school, after a trip to Central Park, to what she had learned from Dunn:

> I remember one day one of the little boys said, "You all sit there and watch me." He had a tin can on a string, and he climbed up on this rock with it. Then he dropped it, making it bounce against the side of the big rock, almost like a puppet. We were just mesmerized watching this tin can. It made me realize that anything can be interesting. And that's what Bob Dunn was teaching us also. I think it's because of Bob that I could see this little event with the tin can as theater, as dance, as working with movement. (Perron 2021)

This ongoing and extensive exploration of play as not only a source of inspiration for dance pieces but in itself a legitimate form of dance is also reflected in Forti's work with animals, her interest in animal movement having begun when she was a child and becoming a particular focus when she lived in Rome in the late '60s. In her time observing animals, as Wendy Perron explains of the game structures Forti devised, "She watched long enough to discern patterns in the walking of the bears, the sparring of the chimps, the diving of otters .... She noticed that some animals, like children, make up games to entertain themselves. She saw bears "whipping their bodies around ... sorta like kids do somersaults or twirl or swing on a swing'" (Perron 2021). Forti also observed and appreciated the playful movements of sea lions, noting, "The sea lions were having great fun. They were really doing movement play, which as far as I'm concerned is one of the roots of dance" (Bryan-Wilson 2015, 36).

While she prioritized natural movements over formalized technique, Forti's *Dance Constructions* and other works also demonstrated that various aspects of a dancer's or a movement artist's performance could be improved with practice. She was interested in the idea of a gesture or response becoming "second nature" through repetition. Like a tennis player going for a tennis ball and hitting it well due to extensive training, over time a dancer's movements could become so familiar and fluid that they could be executed without conscious thought (Morse 2016, 24).

|| And a tra la la
other modes branching

drifted apart.
as both transition. But you
on the balls or toes of the feet. cheerleader
most natural
Quick, even steps,
gliding. || I opened
and closing
a life of routines recitals

dream, not mine

|| "And a couple of tra la las to seek
out other modes branching

drifted *Step of bourrée. Leg extended*
as both transition. But you kept *Rising*
onto the balls of the feet.
Eventually, The most natural thing
inevitability. *Quick, even steps, en pointe, giving*
|| "I opened
But something was off."
a life of routines and recitals no
longer
Years
dictated, all to be watched by others. || "
I was living my friend's dream, not mine.

|| "And a couple of tra la las ...." In junior high, you began to seek out other modes of performance, branching out from dance. At the local community theater, *The Wizard of Oz,* to start. || We attended different high schools, drifted apart. *Step of bourrée. Leg extended, the first closed to the second as both transition.* But you kept dancing. *Rising onto the balls or toes of the feet.* You were a cheerleader — of course. || Eventually, a bachelor's in dance. The most natural thing, it seemed. Almost an inevitability. *Quick, even steps, often en pointe, giving the appearance of gliding.* || "I opened a ballroom dance studio with a friend. But something was off." *The second leg open, and closing the first to the second.* || After a life of routines and recitals, you could no longer ignore the sense of growing unease, that dance felt somehow passive, disempowering. Years doing what a choreographer or director dictated, all to be watched by others. || "After a few months, I realized I was living my friend's dream, not mine. So I quit." ||

Like Forti, Yvonne Rainer was greatly influenced by Anna Halprin's 1960 summer workshop, where she was exposed to Halprin's groundbreaking ideas on natural movement. This is also where Rainer met Trisha Brown, one of the dancers with whom she would go on to found the Judson Dance Theater in New York in 1962. Rainer's work was characterized as a "kind of anti-dance" that emphasized banal movements and non-expression. She was not interested in gratifying her audience, nor in asking them to buy into the "comfy illusion" delivered by modern dance; rather than performative delivery, she sought a "matter-of-fact" style in which the dancer would "'just do it'" (Roy 2010). Indeed, postmodern dance sought to forego the artifice of traditional dance forms and instead involved familiar, pedestrian acts like walking, crouching, and falling, enacted by ordinary bodies in intimate spaces. In Rainer's aptly named *We Shall Run* (1963), for example, the dancers run around the stage for 12 minutes in street clothes, an artistic choice that also illustrates the allowance of levity and playfulness in works of this period (Crawford 2020).[1]

Moreover, the timing of the emergence of postmodern dance, amid transformational artistic and social change — including second-wave feminism — clearly influenced the approach and output of many choreographers, whose work was to some extent about "seeking alternative ways of moving through space and, by extension, life" (Guadagnino 2019). By introducing and achieving acceptance for such new, unexpected types of movement, these artists could challenge the way women's bodies were controlled and mistreated, underscoring the legitimacy of women's search for greater freedom.

Rainer's work consistently and purposefully addresses the importance of maintaining control and objectivity as a female artist, to counter objectification of dancers' bodies. Regarding her piece *Duet* (1963), in which she and Brown wore tights and black lace push-up bras, Rainer doing ballet while Brown performed a mixture of ballet and burlesque, Rainer acknowledged her attraction to experiencing power over her audience during performance. At the time, she believed this sensation was necessary for the audience to be taken in by the artist's presence. But within just a couple of years, she was renouncing erotic aspects of performing that she had enjoyed enacting in her choreography and raging "against forms of dancing that she felt were disguised sexual exhibitionism" (Burt 2006, 73–74).

As she states in an interview published in *The Paris Review*, discussing her dance *Trio A* (1967):

1 YVONNE RAINER: *We Shall Run* has always been performed by performers of both genders and has never had anything to do with "the way women's bodies are controlled and mistreated!" Jesus!

AUTHOR: An earlier version of this essay was edited in such a way that implied that *We Shall Run* addressed the issue of control and mistreatment of women's bodies. This connection was inaccurate and has been corrected to better reflect Rainer's intention with this piece.

> I began to question my own enjoyment and what I term a kind of narcissism and pleasure in being looked at as a performer. The symbiotic relation of being looked at, and looking, seemed to reinforce this kind of exhibitionism. [...] So I refused to look at the audience. Rather, the gaze becomes inward. I'm either looking at my own body or anticipating where a part of my body is going to go or, if my body faces the audience, I give special movements for my head like rolling around as the body moves sideways across the space. Or, after having just done a backward somersault, I come up with my eyes closed. (Storr 2017)

Rainer subsequently turned her focus to film, where she found more opportunity to deepen her attention on the subject (what the viewer reads) rather than the object (what the viewer sees) (Roy 2019). Discussing her 1985 film *The Man Who Envied Women*, she describes how she circumvented objectification of the body to facilitate female empowerment through her treatment of the female character, Tricia:

> In my piece I take her physical presence out of the picture. I was influenced by critiques of the oversexualization of women in Hollywood movies and so I said to myself, "Okay, I'll take her out totally, and she'll be a controlling voice," since very often in film noir a man's voice is the controlling voice. (Storr 2017)

After many years away from dance, Rainer returned to the form in 2000, when Mikhail Baryshnikov invited her to choreograph for his White Oak Dance project, noting, "I've come back to the body as the main element of my work. Once a dancer, always a dancer, I suppose" (Josephs 2009).

To neutralize what is personal: Fabricate a space with deconstructed memories, dreams interwoven with other realities, reconstructed. Connections made strange, as leaps in our daily lives.

*Modes of resistance or ways to return to a childlike state: Move to surpass learned syntax, conventions of grammar. Avoid mold-making, casting, cultivating complicity. Disregard patterning, how words *should* appear on the page.*

To awaken one's artistic sensibility: Mimic structures that call to mind "the generalized response of infants" (Forti 1998, 34). Explore play to circumvent expectation. Master dimensioning, to realize a full-figure animal. Understand dance as a series of natural movements — or movements that become second nature.

The benefits of a body de-emphasized: As we practice techniques of manipulation, pulling strings, moderating the presence of the artist. An exercise in projection.

How to design a neutral mask: Reject objectification by replacing ourselves with objects. Devise a model that invites examination of self, filtered. Develop strategies for lifting "an emotional load" (Koch 1972, 58). Rooted in the playful, the physical, the performer-creator.

Forti's piece *Cloths* (1967) involves the use of song recordings and live singing, three performers obscured behind square frames holding pieces of cloth. The participants intermittently flip the cloths from behind the frame to the front, until they've all been turned. This idea of hiding behind some kind of object or prop arose from a very personal place; it had "come from a disquieting dream: the person she was married to didn't want to see her any longer, so she had to hide 'behind furniture, in closets' in their apartment" (Morse 2016, 60). But Forti avoided drawing clear linkages to her own experience; in this piece and other early works, she sought to moderate the presence of the performer, making the voice "a bodily surrogate, a 'ghost' [...] unattached to an actual, visible body" (Morse 2016, 119).

In a way, this parallels what Rainer did later in film; both found ways to avoid objectification by emphasizing the voice rather than the body. Forti routinely devised methods to separate the performer's body — initially, at least, *her* body — from the voice that spread outward in a space. By creating distance between body and voice through various tactics, she purposefully tempered the autobiographical associations of personal material, in much the same way a ventriloquist might use a "surrogate" body as a way to take the focus off them, thereby altering the viewer's experience of a performance (Morse 2016, 113).

In Forti's *Cloths* and *Platforms* (1961) — which involves two performers whistling from within boxes — the performers are unseen and thus deemphasized, and both pieces include voice elements that prompt the viewer to associate the human voice with an object (the cloths and the wooden boxes, respectively). "An object made to stand in for a performer precisely where visual or aural cues might demand a body — as a puppet of sorts — becomes an emphatically blank presence; such a blankness might effectively neutralize an otherwise unacceptable emotive load" (Morse 2016, 120).

With these kinds of approaches, artists could more freely incorporate personal material into their work without sentimentalizing their experiences or drawing attention to themselves as subjects. They could use images from their dreams or personal lives and still maintain the sense of neutrality and objectivity they sought. And *Cloths*, especially, demonstrates an embrace, an enactment, of a sort of puppetry: the performers interacting with the set and props, themselves not visible to the audience. In full control of the action and hidden from view, neither they nor their bodies can be objectified — a sensation further heightened when Forti herself is one of the performers. In other words: they are pulling the strings.

The beginning of an ongoing conversation

a portal to enter
dancing

behind beloved characters

I thought
my dance
background uniquely
To land *standing*. I
thought I thought Then
Thrown *sideways*. ||

at ArtMart I wanted
I wanted to be

"And I just started
an ongoing conversation
enabling *craft.*
|| *Being John Malkovich,*
a portal to enter and control the mind

and after "I wanted to
pull the strings." || *To turn,* *the leading leg, the body*

behind beloved characters — Mr. Snuffleupagus

what I needed
"With my dance
background, I felt I was
To land with the leading leg standing. I
thought my audition I thought Then
Thrown. In the direction of a movement, sideways. ||

|| "I got a job at ArtMart because I wanted to know more about all types of art. I wanted to be around artists, learn from them. When one day, in walks Bob Kramer." Founder of one of the longest-running puppetry theaters in the country. "And I just started talking to him." The beginning of an ongoing conversation about his work, ultimately leading to an apprenticeship, enabling you to learn about his craft. || Also around this time, you happened to see *Being John Malkovich*, about a puppeteer who accesses a portal to enter and control the mind of the actor John Malkovich. You'd come to view dancing as akin to being a puppet — and after a lifetime of being directed: "I wanted to pull the strings." || *To turn, with the leading leg, the body 180 degrees.* While working with Kramer, you joined the Puppet Guild of St. Louis. Attended puppetry conferences, workshops taught by well-known puppeteers behind beloved characters — Mr. Snuffleupagus from "Sesame Street" and others. You applied for a Master's in Puppetry at the University of Connecticut, the only such program in the country. "I thought this was what I needed to do to pursue this as a career." || Observed the other candidates at the audition. "With my dance background, I felt I was uniquely qualified. The other applicants didn't have that." *The other leg brushing. To land with the leading leg standing.* I thought my audition went well. I thought I'd get in." Then you didn't. *Thrown. In the direction of a movement, sideways.* ||

In preparing to write this essay, to represent the memory of my relationship with my childhood best friend, Angela, I decided to enact some of the ballet moves whose names she spoke so often: *plié, pas de bourrée, tour jeté.* The words themselves had been etched into my mind primarily through her frequent repetitions of them, absent of meaning. Perhaps by studying them, developing some kind of intellectual and physical understanding of these terms, I could get a little closer to what her practice, what these movements — which had been etched into her body through the magic of muscle memory — meant to her.

With just a brief YouTube tutorial to guide me, my "performances" were rudimentary (that's an understatement). But quality of execution wasn't the point. I wanted to return to that period, to recall time spent at her house, at the playground, observing her at play. Because, while I always admired Angela's technical skill, what I appreciated more was her ability to incorporate her own style and sensibility into what she did, much in the way H'Doubler, Halprin, Forti, and Rainer spoke of — and enacted. Her commitment to being true to herself, infusing her work with joy and playfulness, was inspiring and came through in her dancing, and later, in her puppetry. Early on she'd embraced the world of formal dance, but like these postmodern artists, she came to reject its constraints; above all else, she wanted to maintain control. She resisted objectification and manipulation because she wanted to pull the strings — and have fun doing it. Ultimately, she didn't continue with puppetry, but she wasn't subject to anyone else's vision, either.

Over the years I, too, developed an interest in puppetry. Most notably, in high school I took a puppetry class in which we worked in groups to write our own plays, build puppets and sets, and perform for local elementary schools. The goals were to construct a "moving mouth," master character design, and realize a full-figure animal. In my play, Em and M embark on a quest to save the native chocolate trees from destruction. To do so, they must journey through the Caramel Bog and overcome various harrowing travails, with help from the Three Musketeers they encounter along the way. I became practiced in manipulation, patterning, dimensioning. My characters were lively, animated, and utterly at ease with their movements. They were possessed with the bodily confidence I've always lacked, an exercise in projection. This the only time my drama teacher didn't criticize the quality of my facial expressions. A fabricated scenario is less easily denied. I learned to awaken natural movement, giving voice and action to my characters. A way to maintain a certain degree of comfort. Control. A vehicle by which to employ kinesthetic awareness, in a sense. Invisible to the audience, precluding the possibility of physical objectification or critique.

As a writer, I engage primarily with the abstract world of ideas, of words. Yet I've also long been drawn to art grounded in the physical world, and sought to develop an expansive and inclusive practice, which often involves a multiplicity of mediums and methodologies, as well as a variety of collaborators of different genres and aesthetics. To that end, I've experimented with collage, collecting and reformulating fragments from maps, sci-fi novels, conversations overheard on a train, sometimes cutting lines into strips of paper and rearranging them on a table, observing how words *do things* we can't apprehend upon first laying them on a screen or a page. I fold in slivers of autobiographical content — possibilities revealing themselves through a combination of serendipity and calculation. Probing gaps and overlaps. I build structures to house my adopted/adapted words, altering punctuation and form to bolster my constructions. I've recorded soundscapes, audio tracks layered, to create correspondences of language, voice. Meaning as salient as sound. I've interwoven my own language with that of other writers and artists, worked with dancers and performance artists whom I admire for their ability to engage with human experience on a somatic level. I've partnered with sound and visual artists, who can dimensionalize work in ways not possible with the written word alone. Through these collaborations, I strive to embrace the push and pull of maintaining control versus letting go, to arrive at unexpected juxtapositions, alignments, and tensions. Sometimes we want to pull the strings; sometimes we need another set of hands to extend our reach.

More than ever, in writing this essay, I've come to appreciate unexpected, unconventional methods — including play — as a means to break out of habit, create something new. The importance, the imperative, of a female artist to maintain control and ownership of work, to forge her own way in her chosen art form — however she defines it. What true collaboration and an openness to other ways of art-making can bring to one's practice. And how all this can be done in innumerable ways — through theater and dance, visual art and music, as well as through writing. There are many ways to play.

Notes

Italicized ballet terms are from Wikipedia, s.v. "Glossary of Ballet," https://en.wikipedia.org/wiki/Glossary_of_ballet.

Puppetry terms appearing in the central italicized section and recurring at the end of the essay are based on the course titles and descriptions from *University of Connecticut School of Fine Arts* (n.d.).

The line "Connections made strange, as leaps in our daily lives" is inspired by Forti's description of "strange jumps" in Forti (2015), her interview with Alessandra Nicifero for the Robert Rauschenberg Oral History Project.

Quotes that appear throughout the text blocks are by Angela Hoffman from a phone call with the author in July 2018.

"And a couple of tra la las ..." is from the song "The Merry Old Land of Oz" from the film *The Wizard of Oz* (Arlen 1939).

COLLABORATION IN MOTION

We (Valerie and Sarah) arrived at our focus on Forti and Rainer through a combination of intention and happy accident. When we were seeking to devise a joint writing project in 2016, we came across a chapbook called *Eternal Apprentice,* a collaboration between Michael Newton and Emmalea Russo (2016). We were drawn to the lively yet thoughtful dance between these two minds. The dialogue included a reference to Cage and Cunningham's use of chance operations to generate art that circumvents the artist's habit or will—a methodology we had both dabbled in and wanted to explore further. We were troubled by the fact that we were so much more familiar with the work of these two lionized men than with the women artists whom their work helped inspire. We realized that researching the work of the latter might lead to a compelling focus for our project. Valerie associated dance with experiences of failure and discomfort while Sarah approached it primarily as a zone of grace and joy; we recognized that this contrast would add another dimension to our collaboration and allow a range of readers to see themselves reflected in it.

We each selected an artist to research: Valerie chose Simone Forti and Sarah chose Yvonne Rainer. Based on that research we wrote a book, *The Grass Is Greener When the Sun Is Yellow.* The project created a dynamic collaborative relationship, expanding our respective practices in a way poet Norma Cole (2009) captured well when describing the appeal of collaboration: "You become startlingly aware of your 'habits,' your practice. You can then try to change course, follow different tracks, traces. At times, you become one with the other person for the duration of the work; so you become another being, a dyad." At the same time, it kindled our desire to engage more deeply with Forti's and Rainer's work and to excavate our own relationships to dance in light of these artists' ideas.

Fire and Flood: Enacting Rehearsal as Performance

Sarah Rosenthal

Dear Yvonne Rainer,

Today I guest-taught a friend's undergraduate creative writing class at the California College of the Arts. The task was to help the students prepare to write their creative nonfiction essays. I employed as a basis an essay I wrote about the relationship between Simone Forti's use of kinesthetic awareness in her dances and my own memories of studying ballet. Drawing on the elaborate process I used to write that essay, I had devised a procedure for helping the students generate their own essays. At a brisk clip, they did free-writes to prompts; wrote words on slips of paper they folded and gave to others, who shook the slips in paper cups before selecting them for one another; talked through ideas with partners; brainstormed as a group. In the middle of it all, I guided them through Anna Halprin's community-building activity: stand in a circle, say your name and where you live, make a gesture, then we all mirror that back to you. After our ninety minutes together, I invited them to send me their completed essays, then headed back into the atmosphere shaggy with smoke on day seven of the Camp Fire raging in Butte County.

I stood during most of my visit. The tables were high and the chairs ergonomically disastrous, but besides that, standing seemed like an aid to conducting the energy so that, within a short time, I could help a bunch of strangers take a meaningful journey.

The session felt theatrical but not because I was standing, or not entirely. I didn't feel I was doing a solo act but rather that everyone in the room was performing our encounter. Maybe I was picking up on the way art students tend to bring a performative quality to life. Even the quiet types are accustomed to peers' antics and displays. Before class, out in the courtyard, I'd watched an impromptu Happening: Two students froze and mirrored each other's flung-open arms, a third joined, they all looked at each other expectantly, and then one initiated a wild dance the other two mimicked. Moments later, the wild one taught the whole sequence to two other friends.

So by the time I entered the class, it was obvious the four white walls were a set and we were all there to act our parts. The students were mostly engaged, occasionally laconic. A few were unadorned; others wore neon pink, orange, and green, which made them look like fruit. Or fruit-flavored Halloween candy, sugary and bright. The shaped eyebrows of the girl in the brown T-shirt to my right were boats rocking. I recognized Rocking Boat Girl, she's my dream daughter, the one I forgot to raise, fully formed now, not harmed by my neuroses, at least not blatantly, what a relief, although I'm not sure I get to take pride. Did the fact that she had boats on her face mean the hoop earrings of the boy across the room were lifesavers? I needed one when suddenly the students went mute. Had I phrased my question poorly? Were they getting tired? Hungry? I wrote on the whiteboard: *taste, sight, smell, touch.* "Um, what am I missing?" Someone said, "Sound." "Yes, sound. And you know I'm going to write *kinesthetic awareness,*" I said, scribbling.

No doubt another reason I saw a performative element in that ninety minutes has to do with my day job. Since the mid-'00s I've spent part of my time working at an education nonprofit designing language arts curricula. We build open-ended questions, facilitation techniques, and classroom management tips into the lessons to help teachers maximally engage students while honing their own professional chops. I've often described what we do as helping turn ordinary US classrooms into something akin to graduate seminars where students express their unique perspectives while listening deeply to one another. Although some of the art students were barely out of high school, I was eager, as I am whenever I find myself teaching post-secondary populations, to test how this pedagogy for younger students applies and how it might improve upon the way I taught writing to college kids and older populations before joining the nonprofit. This goal alone would have intensified my experience that day.

On a more intuitive level, my perception of my time with the students as a performance was also fed by recent reflections on the work you've done to cross the line between preparation for a performance and the performance itself. I'd been musing about the 1970 Whitney Museum staging of your piece *Continuous Project — Altered Daily,* in which you included "the range of situations that normally occur prior to performance: teaching, social interaction, working out of new material, conversation, and other rehearsal-like situations" (Lambert-Beatty 2008, 203). Simone Forti reminisces about "Tea for Two," a 1980 talk the two of you gave: "[W]e had a little round table with a teapot and our two cups. We started talking fifteen minutes before the audience was able to come in so by the time they came in, we were going" (Forti 2015, 22). In or around 2002, a video was made of you performing a comical attempt to teach your iconic dance *Trio A* to Martha Graham impersonator Richard Move. In your in-progress work *The Concept of Dust, or How Do You Look When There's Nothing Left to Move?* the dancers must each find a way to hang out onstage while audience members arrive, before shifting into the "real" performance (Rainer 2015a).

Why present pre-performance activities like teaching as performance? Art historian Carrie Lambert-Beattie suggests that your doing so demonstrates an interest, shared by some of your peers, in interrupting time and displacing space (2008, 212). This breaks our habituated way of viewing art and offers a more exciting possibility (Lambert-Beatty 2008, 209). What's perplexing and endlessly fascinating to me is that this visionary possibility you offer is nothing more or less than our own lives. The utopian space you create onstage has incorporated elements like untrained dancers along with professionals; ordinary objects such as pillows and cardboard boxes; and people interacting as they do pedestrian tasks and activities like dragging things, running, and resting. Beginning early in your career, you have worked to dismantle implicit tenets of forms ranging from classical ballet to modern dance and even Happenings — tenets you saw as severely limiting dance's potential (Rainer 1965).

Over time I'm feeling pervaded, invaded, poisoned maybe, by a yen for process, and I think my investigation of your work is amplifying this condition. I have trouble lately distinguishing what part of the art-making is the art. These words addressed to you are part of a project so elaborate that without referring to notes I can't even describe all the steps my collaborator Valerie Witte and I invented, incorporating chance and dance to arrive at the subject matter for each essay. What I did with the students was a mere soupçon. We set up our project that way because we wanted to feel as close to you, Simone Forti, and your peers as we could. We wanted to turn you into mentors by inhabiting your chutzpah, your resistance to the status quo. We wanted to circumvent intentionality — get out of our own way — to think and see and say things we'd never thought or seen or said. And we wanted to get so caught up in play we forgot we were working.

Whenever I speak of play in this way, I recall a conversation I had with a poet a number of years ago, while she and I were editing an interview I'd done with her. I had called her work playful. She said, "Cut that word, it describes what children do, it doesn't communicate the heft of my art." I felt a little resentful because "playful" was a word I often applied to her work, and I considered it a positive attribute. But I could see how, from her perspective, it felt wrong. She came of age, as you did, in a period when women artists had to fight to be taken seriously. Given that context, I saw that she might well experience the word "playful" as diminishing and infantilizing, in a gender-laden way. I removed it.

Yet in my own art, I'm working to reclaim play — and no doubt I can entertain this precisely because she, you, and many others have carved out a space where I can do so without fearing erasure. I've often tended toward a drudge-like, fear-based approach to art-making, which I can trace to a childhood in which I did not have the luxury of enough play. There was too much to monitor in my environment, too much trouble to stay out of or be implicated in. There were too many hurt people to try to help and too many secret worries about what a bad job of being a person I seemed to be doing. So over time I turn ever more toward play. Absorption in process rather than concern about outcomes feels like play to me. Messing with received notions of "the warm-up versus the finished product" feels like play. Experiencing connection and community via gamelike proceedings and collaborative projects seems a better focus than striving to earn accolades. I'm not at all done with the latter, but making my own fun seems preferable, overall, to waiting for thunderous applause to erupt from the dark out there beyond the stage lights.

I'm not sure where you stand on the concept of play. You and your peers have dealt a lot with the concept of work, having dancers do ordinary, task-like activities. In *The Concept of Dust,* I can see both work-like and play-like elements (Rainer 2015a). But after my experience with the poet, I'm cautious about reading the word "play" into women's art unless they claim it themselves. At any rate, process is central to both work and play. And given that I'm more focused than ever on process these days, it inevitably dominated my approach with the art students.

Another key influence on my teaching that day was the idea of transmission. Asking an audience, as you have done, to watch as one teaches one's choreography to a group of individuals, is a way of asserting the importance of the act of transmission. Such an activity highlights the seriousness of intent, the dedication on both the teacher's and learner's parts, the intimacy required and engendered. You've continued to transmit your work to others over time, notably through the teaching of *Trio A* to dancers and, early on, to people who lacked dance training.[1] You've done this through your own teaching and that of a small cadre of dancers you've trained. Catherine Wood points out that this transmission creates a gift economy that in a small but potent way challenges capitalism. (Wood notes that these days, you and your appointed teachers receive payment for the teaching, and you receive a royalty whenever *Trio A* is performed, so it's no longer a pure gift economy [2007, 96–100]. I hear Wood's point, but also reflect that we all live inside a capitalist structure and have to support ourselves. This is such a thorny topic: how we as artists stay true to our values. We all need more intellectual honesty as we figure this out. I'd love to hear how you're navigating capitalism currently, since I know you've done a lot of thinking about this over time.) Julia Bryan-Wilson, who through comical happenstance found herself shedding her heady art-historian persona and not only learning the dance from you but also performing it, describes a process both humbling — at one point during the class you asked her, "Do you even know how to run?" — and transformative (2012, 59).

When I was preparing for and then teaching the art students, it felt like a transmission too. Having devised a procedure for generating essays based on my experience as an experimental poet and pedagogue as well as other artists' use of chance operations, I was sharing that procedure in condensed form. The brisk set of paces I walked the students through was intended to defamiliarize writing, activating new ways of being and seeing. It might seem like I thought of the students as racehorses or marionettes, but the steps I taught were intended as an offering to artists-in-training, a choreography they might choose over time to incorporate pieces of, or to reject whole cloth. Something was happening that was more than just

1 YVONNE RAINER: I agree with your assessment of "play" — Again, I no longer teach *Trio A* to non-dancers or allow people who learn it on their own from the 1967 video to perform it, if I can help it —
AUTHORS: As with all references to *Trio A* in the collection, this one has been revised to make clear that Rainer no longer endorses the teaching of the dance to nondancers.

preparing them to write their essays (a kind of performance for which they will receive louder or softer applause in the form of a grade). It was a gift economy, a sharing, that was in and of itself, for me, "the thing."

None of this is what I had planned to write. I'd intended to describe a performance collaborative I participated in some years ago, called diSh. But perhaps we can take a breath before that happens, since breathing is one of the things we share.

Yours,

Sarah

Dear Yvonne,

I'm home in my study writing this, as safe as anyone can be these days, yet something in me is terrified. I want to smother that feeling by trimming my nails or attacking dust bunnies or eating chocolate or roaming the internet looking for a reflection of myself.

I'm putting myself on the line here, claiming that this is an essay, which implies some kind of coherence, while wanting to sprawl into my associational-poet mind. I'm trying to tell myself that the epistolary form is capacious enough to hold all this. But the letter form introduces another vulnerability, that of addressing you directly. What if you are bored or irritated by what I write — or worse, feel misrepresented? What if I'm perceived as self-aggrandizing by framing this as a kind of correspondence with you, even if one-sided?

Of course, I could end up deleting this self-exposing admission or anything else I write here. No one would be the wiser. But it seems to me the challenge of this essay is to take up the invitation you gave and keep giving: to trust that the pre-work can be part of the final piece. To claim that the process of making art can at times *be* the art. To find a way to welcome the messy and the vulnerable.

I have no intention of abandoning the recursiveness and editability of the writing process. That particular aspect of the complex relationship to time that print inhabits is one of writing's greatest gifts. But at the same time, I want to lean into the way live performance marks time — or rather, I want to lean into your and your peers' revolutionary experiments with the traditional configuration of performance time, in a way that reveals the ordinary, flawed, constantly morphing beauty of us.

These characters manifesting on the page are dancers who don't know the difference between rehearsal and performance. If someone told them, "It will all be a rehearsal forever," they would nod and continue their combinations. If someone said, "It's a performance from the word go," they would wipe the sweat from their foreheads and keep moving.

Regards,

Sarah

Dear Yvonne,

I hope you are doing well, at your home in New York City, far from the fires that continue to rage here in California. My teaching gig the other day was infused with thoughts of you. But back in the late '90s, when I co-founded a performance ensemble with two poets I met in grad school at San Francisco State, I hadn't heard of you and your peers — though by that point you'd been working for decades, had in fact long since segued from dance to film and were just then returning to dance. That said, Merce Cunningham, your teacher of eight years, along with John Cage, whose ideas you were also steeped in, helped inspire that ensemble.

Fellow MFA student Rose and I attended a performance by Cunningham's company at UC Berkeley's Zellerbach Hall. We barely knew each other — we were in a seminar together, got to chatting, made the plan. Another poet tagged along, but it was Rose I was drawn to: her physical grace, her ability to shift easily from quiet witness to raucous clown, the mysterious beauty and depth of the haibuns she'd been writing, the seeming ease with which she combined her background as a Gestalt therapist with avant-garde poetics. Psychology was a no-no in experimental writing; I admired her willingness to go against the tide. And I was entranced by the luminous performance that night — athletic dancers with neutral expressions skimming the stage like dragonflies, accompanied by musicians playing Cage's score on high platforms erected around the periphery of the square stage, so that the presence of the orchestra felt both ethereal and like workers building something.

Around that time another student in our cohort, Dana, returned to school after an illness that had nearly killed her. In the wake of that experience, she seemed more available for contact. Cracked open, it seemed to Rose, it seemed to me, as we separately found ourselves forming friendships with her. Why not make it a triangle, let more sparks fly? We started sending each other our dreams, wondering where that might lead. When Dana created a biannual performance series called Link, which required participants to collaborate on ten-minute works outside their usual art form, our ensemble diSh was born, and the dream-sharing activity became the basis of our first piece.

Between us, we had just enough theater background for the idea of creating performances to seem risky yet doable. Poetry formed our bridge to gesture, while a shared desire to create an enriching, nurturing process gave us a net. For that ten-minute piece, we spent four weekends at Rose's house in San Rafael in what amounted to our own performance lab. We wrote, brainstormed, played theater games, improvised, and conferred, gradually shaping a piece that included solo and group sections. We didn't have anything resembling a worked-out poetics of performance, but we did have the determination to use every resource at our disposal. At one point we all admitted to feeling competitive with one another, and Rose said, "Let's put that energy to work." The result was a section in which we advanced slowly toward the audience, elbowing each other out of the way as we tried to outdo one another in telling the most attention-grabbing story (dream fragments, but we didn't name them as such), our non sequiturs building a cockeyed narrative. At one point I recounted how a man took advantage of my generosity and I repeated, "Just go then! Just go!" Dana interrupted: "But inside the plane, things were a little rocky." That got an appreciative laugh on the night of the performance and was emblematic of our effort to listen deeply to one another and to our emerging material.

Although moments like that might have come across as improvisatory, the improv feel was a lucky leftover. Acutely aware of our amateur abilities, we wanted to do all we could to ensure high performance values, and once we landed on the contours of the piece, we rehearsed the hell out of it. But we also shared the conviction that feeding ourselves, both literally and figuratively, would help us do our best work. So our weekends were punctuated with tea and feasts (I can still taste Rose's signature salad of pears, mint, and maple syrup), breaks for swaying in the patio hammock, and even a trip to a local spa.

Recently I was telling my partner, who has a background in theater, about how you've done teaching and rehearsals as performance. He said, "That makes so much sense, because the pre-work is sometimes the best part — everyone feels acutely alive, committed, part of something being born. They're trying stuff out, building these intense relationships." In the case of diSh, I can't say the development process was better than the performances themselves — the latter gave us an incredible adrenaline rush. But it's a toss-up, for sure. Those weekends were juicy. Utopian.

We built our next and, as it turned out, last piece around Dana's expressed desire to do a striptease. Her then-fiancé had found himself at a bachelor-party stripper act and hadn't resisted the experience the way she would have hoped. She was grappling with her complicated feelings — hurt, anger, fear of being labeled a prude — and as one response wanted to reclaim the sensuality of the classic striptease, to the tune of "Where the Boys Are," stopping short of nudity. She pictured it as a possible starting point of a piece that would interrogate women's relationship to our sexuality and our deeply enculturated, misguided attempts to get love and approval. I felt threatened, both by the fact that she had such a clearly articulated concept (I wanted to do another performance but felt lost when it came to drumming up interesting material for it) and by the concept of a striptease itself — it went against every feminist bone in my body as well as my long history of sexual repression. But another part of me wanted to say yes to Dana's idea and use it as a point of departure for potentially risk-taking and important work. Finally, I found a way to embrace it, by enacting the opposite. Dana envisioned her section as a joyful, invitational performance, replete with elbow-length gloves and other femme accoutrements peeled off and tossed over the top of a screen before she appeared, shimmying and shaking, winsome and alluring in red lingerie and fishnets. I conceived a horrific, concentration-camp-inmate inversion of that: I grossly exaggerated the stereotypic gestures and facial expressions of seduction, tearing at my ragged clothes, a starving, traumatized woman desperately trying to remember from one moment to the next the cannon of striptease gestures that might keep the audience entertained, earning me another day of life.

I was accompanied by an almost unbearably screechy recording by Miya Masaoka and Fred Frith. Rose planned to conclude the piece with a healing, goddessy monologue and dignified, sweeping gestures that conveyed womanhood as a state of both fluidity and strength.[2]

The pre-performance work went fine — theater games, pear salads, hammock breaks, the works — till Rose asserted that Dana's ten-minute rule for all Link performers should not apply to us. In particular, she wanted more time for her own section. Dana and I resisted. Rose persisted, saying, "I get rushed all the time by this culture. I will not let that happen to my art."

Finally, Dana agreed to a few extra minutes. We continued with rehearsals, and the performance went well. But the fight left a sour taste, and our group disbanded. My relationship with Rose fizzled. Dana's did too, though many years later.

Not everything ends on a happy note. I'll write again tomorrow. I hope by then I'll have figured out how to justify taking your time with this story.

Till then,

Sarah

Dear Yvonne,

In your 2017 conversation with Lynne Tillman at Lincoln Center, she said, "Experience is one thing and art is another." You responded, "Well, not in my life" (Rainer 2017a). Your response describes exactly what I'm — I was going to write, "up against." But why am I picturing this situation as something to be up against, rather than as something simply to inhabit?

I won't kid you, I'm struggling with this essay. My life and my art are happening at the same moment and it's not feeling easy and why?

Let me try to name what I am thinking of as "my problem."

I am trying to execute the plan for this essay, which was to investigate your — what shall I call it — your adventure — your adventurous presentation to audiences of what is usually framed as the preparation for performance (which is just one small enactment of your always-evolving poetics) and somehow relate it to my experience as a member of diSh. That plan abides by the constraints of this essay project, using chance and memories of dance to arrive at the new. I honor that commitment, that limit.

But I find myself wanting to talk about all kinds of things I didn't intend to include here. I'm thinking about *Calamities*, a book of essays by Renee Gladman, which I just finished a few minutes ago and which closely investigates the act of writing and its relationship to living, which reminds me of how Leslie Scalapino described both her and Bernadette Mayer's investigation of the same relationship: "It's such a heightened attention to the *act* of attention, that that [*sic*] then transforms what happens" (Scalapino 2010, 282). I'm picturing these three writers in a room, each at their own desk but breathing common air, trying to inhabit the complex relationship

2 YVONNE RAINER: Fascinating!

between writing and living. That in turn leads me to muse on the connection of all of three to Gertrude Stein, which then triggers my memory of Gladman's grief, expressed during her keynote at the 2018 &Now Festival of New Writing, that Stein does not make a breathable space for Black people in her writing; Gladman said she wanted to have been loved by Stein.

As I sit with these memories, I keep thinking there is some overlap between these artists' investigation of the relation of writing to living, and your investigation of the relation between pre-performance and performance.

Most of the essays in Gladman's book start with the phrase "I began the day," which sounds diaristic, as though she is stirring the flotsam and jetsam, the jewels and treasures of the day, into this writing, which is above all about writing. (It's also about drawing, but for Gladman, drawing is a form of writing. And maybe writing is a form of drawing too.) When a book foregrounds the diurnal in this way, the reader may well wonder how much the writing has been edited before publication. If the book is really a diary — if the writing and the living really are one thing — then once she lay the pen down, was the writer done? But that strikes me as being, frankly, none of my business. There are more interesting questions. For example: What does it do to one's mind to know that writing has elements of both rehearsal and performance in it? To know that it's a performance marked by traces of rehearsal?

Musing on this is feeling more alive to me than squeezing out a comparison between your ideas and diSh. Just as the other day, thinking about that workshop with the art students and its relationship to your work also felt more acute than my initial plan for this essay. But I'm not even willing to hunker down at this new intersection. I'm not willing to say, "My topic has shifted and that's OK, the focus of this essay can shift to accommodate it, especially given the epistolary form's accommodation of nonlinear thinking." That would still be too orderly. I'm being flooded and not feeling willing or able to clean up the mess. I'm so glad for the rain, which is clearing up the air heavily polluted by the Camp Fire that started fourteen days ago, so grateful that I along with millions of others can take a deep breath, that the firefighters can finally get help from nature to extinguish the flames so the destruction can halt and the enormous work of healing destroyed lives, homes, and habitats can begin. But this morning I drove across town to sit in a room for an hour with a person so absorbed in painful thoughts, I wondered if what I was bearing witness to was increasing growth and freedom emerging from the midst of struggle, or instead, ongoing struggle with no break on the horizon. I judged them for their gloomy mood, then judged myself for casting aspersions. When I got home, a woman waiting at the bus stop near my parking spot was crying softly; she couldn't open her umbrella without fear of dropping her cane. The cold rain that's saving lives and lungs was drenching and chilling her. We got her umbrella open and I noticed her perfectly applied, pearly pink lipstick, told her how lovely. She smiled — a moment's respite. Then the bus arrived and she began to tremble. Climbing aboard and getting situated (bless the patient bus driver) was an ordeal. The bus pulled away. Maybe the warm, dry ride to her destination soothed. Maybe not.[3]

I am carrying these people with me now. I am writing them into this piece. I want to hereby make them famous if becoming famous equals receiving love, which very often it doesn't, but asserting that equal sign could become a project, an intervention.

Despite a part of me that admires the tidy, this rain is pouring out of the sky and flooding everything. I want to weep, add to the torrent. Stinging, salty tears, grateful tears, milky tears, buckets of pure water. Regardless of whether you would engage in such an outpouring (though you did make quite a scene, as it were, when you screamed and thrashed around in your 1962 *Three Seascapes* piece), I think you might be able to translate my state into your own determination to scramble, to pile on, to show the sometimes chafed surfaces and the sometimes murky depths (Rainer 2006, 221). To exhibit yourself running rehearsals or teaching your dances in a way that I gather is both caring and, as you have said more than once, controlling (Rainer 2006, 275, and Rainer 2015b). To present not only the thrilling aspects of winnowing and shaping that are part of rehearsal but also perhaps the tedium, the awkward parts, the failures. And to say, this is art. It's my life, and it's my art. I think that, like my current state, your work is beyond the intersection and closer to the flood. I think the flood is there, for example, in your statement about what your work resists: "You will ask, resistance to what? It almost doesn't matter. Resistance to previously imposed canons of taste, to imperialism, to patriarchy, to social inequity, to war, to Abstract Expressionism, you name it. However wrong-headed, misguided, naive, ineffectual, enraged, sublimated — a thread is there" (Wood 2007, 58). This isn't the flood of destruction, the kind that wipes away all the deviants and constructs a narrow ark to save select binaries, two of this and two of that. Sometimes it's the flood of resistance, not unlike when people spill en masse into public spaces to say no to state-sanctioned violence. At times it's the flood of overwhelm, a response to the too-muchness of contemporary life that is unmanageable yet must be at least nominally managed if one isn't to become frenzied or catatonic. And at times it's the flood of bounty, of generosity.[4]

Sometimes I think every work of art is ultimately pointing toward a utopia, even those that focus on the opposite. When you have asked audiences to watch rehearsals and teaching sessions as performance, one implication is that the utopian vision is the here and now. The "should" is the "is." This does not at all mean that the "is" is fine. It simply means, we're alive. Everything matters. Shoulder the pains and tolerate the unknowns. Confront the wrongs. Get to work. Get to play. Let the intimations whisper and shout, the ecstasies spill.

I've let this essay be flooded because we're alive and everything matters. I've allowed the filters and boundaries to dissolve because I trust we're capacious enough to accept and include the rude and the sad, the frightened

---

3 YVONNE RAINER: Woman with umbrella and cane: Nice —

4 YVONNE RAINER: Floods: Nice —

and the broken. Through such release a way forward might emerge, as when the amniotic sac bursts, new life is imminent.

Warm regards,

Sarah

Dear Yvonne,

In the rain.
Of the day.
On the line.
Yours,

Sarah

Note

Dana Teen Lomax provided invaluable help with filling out my memories of diSh.

EXPLORATION, NOT PERSUASION

We were guided to the essay form by the choices we had made in our first book, which comprised collaboratively written sonnets — in which chance operations played a key role — interspersed with letters to one another. Essays felt like a natural next step, a way to deepen our engagement with our topic through a form that invites interrogation and curiosity. Inspired by the audacity of Rainer and Forti, who chose to enter and innovate dance, we wanted to stretch into the essay form while pushing the edges of what it could be.

Of course, in the broader sense, the essay form has made room for risk-taking from the beginning — Michel de Montaigne, credited with its invention in the late sixteenth century, wrote, "My ideas follow one another but sometimes it is from a distance, and look at each other, but with a sidelong glance" (Klaus 1991, 10). Twentieth-century philosopher Theodor Adorno wrote, "The essay's innermost formal law is heresy" (Adorno 1991, 23). In our own time, Jennifer S. Cheng, in a conversation among women writers of color about their engagement with the lyric essay, describes the form as "a way to speak wholeness by speaking holeness, by acknowledging more explicitly the gaps, the silences, the slipperiness of the world" (Cheng 2018). T. Clutch Fleischmann extols non-conventional essayists whose work exhibits formal qualities that "challenge any sense of authoritarianism on the writer's part" (Fleischmann 2013) and Zoë Bossiere observes, "What I love about the lyric essay is that it has this genuine surprise. Anything could happen" (Laing 2023). We wanted to lean into the elasticity of the essay, from experimenting with the basic elements of sentence and paragraph, to splicing scholarly research with poetic lyricism. We have allowed ourselves to raid the storehouses of the established and the radical, from footnotes to line breaks, at will.

Animal Dance: Field Notes for Communicating Outside of Language

Valerie Witte

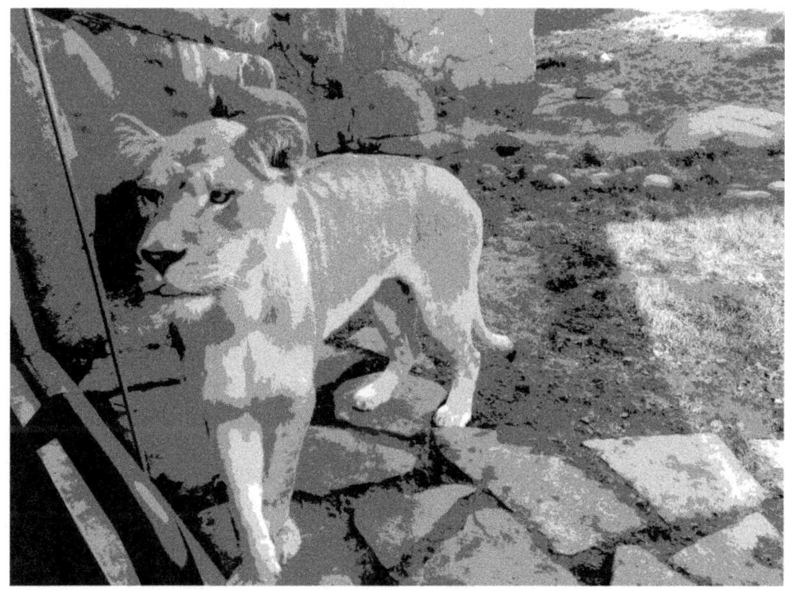

Figure 1. Confined by our walls, whether wire or glass. Dirty or a dance floor. Two surfaces overlaid, framing the activity of their occupants. *(Here was a place made to play, swing and / sway / the most appealing stranger.)* We tell ourselves stories to gauge our range of movement. Our degrees of autonomy vary.* She paces the perimeter, eyeing a lemur in another / enclosure, who too can never escape / its narrative. How we relate to other / our own / bodies. Consider access versus security: what measure. What we must look out for or: a way to behave in schematized spaces.† A place to expose / process / a kind of ongoingness.‡ If what we desire lies beyond reach, why bother? We work with what we have. A selection of themes explored, one for each passage. How to manage containment. Remember, these parallels are limited. Remember, she might pounce. *(I approached without hesitation, shyness shook off: an invitation. We were the only two in that crowd.)*§ A lion captive yet who is protecting whom. What she understands of her circum-

stances‖ / what we salvage, in our cages.¶ Sometimes the difference between inside / outside is nearly indiscernible.

* One distinction between animals and other forms of life is the power to move from place to place, observes zoologist James Gray in the opening of his 1953 book, *How Animals Move.* In zoos, of course, this ability is severely constrained. While in Rome in the late 1960s, Simone Forti studied animals on the streets as well as in the zoo, and her movement studies frequently focused on understanding "gestures of captivity" (Bryan-Wilson 2015, 28).

† Forti's work in the '70s, rooted in the application of "schematized form" and geometric space, aligned with the concerns of process art, which exposed how art was made and the materials with which it was constructed (Morse 2016, 150 and 165). Indeed, various pieces featured performers standing or walking while repeatedly tracing diagonal paths and circles. But within this framework, her attention to the lowered or limited vantage points of lizards or other caged animals also served to "cultivate a radically skewed perspective" and a "new model of perception" of which other artists, especially sculptor Richard Serra, took notice (Morse 2016, 165).

‡ Much of Forti's work was based on the investigations of crawling and circling she'd conducted at the Rome zoo. She often collaborated with sound artists such as Charlemagne Palestine, in whose music the textures "of repetitions and evolving variations are so close that the term melody does not seem to apply. [...] His predominant time sense is a kind of ongoingness." What's most significant is the focus on "immersion" in the process by which art is made (Morse 2016, 150).

§ Forti says, "there's a state of dancing, like there's a state of sleeping, or a state of shivering. Some people have a shyness about entering that state, but everybody does it sometime. Often, at parties, people drop their shyness and enter a dance state. And when I'm in a dance state, the movement that comes out through me enchants me. It can be very simple movement, but it always comes with a sense of wonder, and as one of life's more delicious moments" (Forti 1998, 108).

‖ Presenting the body as a site of both confinement and potential, "Forti takes animal sensations into her own body, embodying animality rather than replicating a situation of captivity." In her dances, "animals are not idealized and romanticized ... but are recognized as beings forced into circumstances beyond their control, constantly mediated by human intervention" (Bryan-Wilson 2015, 46).

¶ "I watched them salvage, in their cages, whatever they could of their consciousness" (Forti 1998, 91).

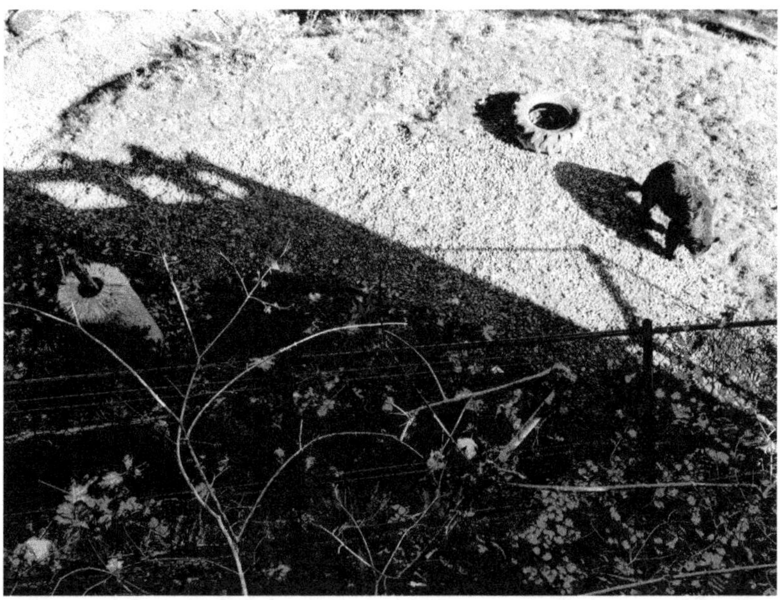

Figure 2. We are all anonymous in certain contexts. Which is preferable / safer / leaves more room for / interpretation. Freedom is not the opposite of vigilance. What we are more or less likely to do with a stranger is anybody's guess. Have I mentioned this essay is about meeting someone at a dance club? Consider the dynamic of observation, watcher or watched. On the prowl, as they say. The animal in this photograph is not a polar bear; I'll explain later. Where the hidden zone of the personal is contained within a public space: how to define this scenario.*† Where two realms intersect, boundaries / blurred. *(Hush Hush.)* I consider adding a new layer of footnotes, facts such as: this was the name of the club. But some details are peripheral, simply unnecessary. *(He was in my immediate field of vision, my attention trained only on him.)* Questions of perspective: how our vantage point dictates what we see / how our gaze inevitably follows an object of desire.‡ *How my body was conditioned to move alongside his, motion as a means of enchantment: a mode of communicating outside language.*§ I tell you how to read me. *(As I read him, his kind, warm smile.)* Today I google him; I still know his face.

❦

* The duality of the personal and the public is a concern explored by many artists during the '60s and '70s, including Forti. In *Cloths* (1967), performers crouch, hidden, behind frames and flip pieces of fabric from front to back, accompanied by live and recorded songs. Based on a dream related to Forti's marriage, *Cloths* offers public presentation while exposing the "hidden zone of the personal" (Morse 2016, 60). As critic Rosalind E. Krauss suggests, the work's blank canvas(es) might serve to signify the "public space of meaning ... as opposed to 'the privacy of psychological space'" of expres-

sionist art, which many artists at the time resisted and sought to supplant with newer movements like Minimalism (quoted in Morse 2016, 60).

† In Trisha Brown's *Roof Piece* (1971), dancers were stationed across a series of SoHo rooftops. A dancer performed a gesture that was repeated by the next dancer and then passed along, north to south and back again, south to north, operating like a game of telephone. Visibility of the piece hinged on "knowledge and access," the first viewing held for friends and colleagues, the second visible only by those on a nearby roof (Morse 2016, 165). The piece actively raised questions regarding the modes of private versus public, welcoming such interrogation and serving as an example of how perspective can shift the impact of a situation, whether real or performative.

‡ When Forti moved like an animal, she could see only what was directly in front of her, "the immediate present" (Morse 2016, 159). This link between temporality and movement is clearly tied to her subjects' lower center of gravity and inability to see beyond the horizon, into the distance. Metaphorically, this limited point of view might also relate to animals' reality of living fully in the present, a mode that humans might aspire to more — one that likely would lead to a greater willingness to take risks.

§ Describing her work *Sleepwalkers/Zoo Mantras* (1969) (alternately known by either name), Forti writes of "a return to movement as a means of enchantment, as in somersaulting down a hill, as a polar bear" (Bryan-Wilson 2015, 39). Regarding the shift in title, critic Julia Bryan-Wilson notes, "as a sacred utterance a mantra points to a realm of communication somewhat outside of normative language, one that, with repetition, leads to greater insight. But who reiterates the 'zoo mantra' to achieve inner calm — the dancer, or the animal?" (2015, 39).

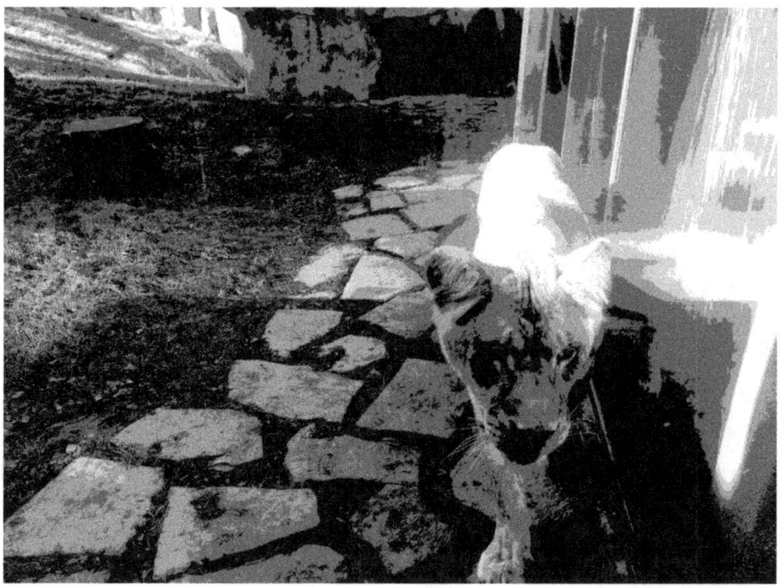

Figure 3. A kind of circling: walk the edge, stop and turn, repeat. These are patterns to settle into and continually replicate.* We try comforting ourselves when there's nothing else / to do. Also: a way of feeling each other / out. *(If he maintained a modest perimeter, I didn't question his reserve.)* So much revolves around circles. *(I did not let him out of my view.)* The degree of focus, persistence required to perform an act over and over without regard to potential "success."† To find comfort in constraints, a way to maintain: we salvage what we can of our consciousness, in our cages. How in dance we default to circles. Patterns settled into, continually / replicated. *(I always believed / the best of him.)* A vague scene replaying in my head: our positions not fixed. *(Yet I recall his back faced the front entrance or exit, depending on perspective. The relationship among our parts shifting fluidly one gesture to the next.)*‡ Now it occurs to me: I've captured the animals in photographs, which Forti would never have done. Or would she? *(Outside after, he kissed my cheeks, a custom not mine. Like a promise. And he called me / angel.)* We are all subject to the laws of gravity. I just hope there isn't an earthquake.

* Forti's animal studies were inspired by the vigor, adaptability, stress, and "occasional joy" of animals who develop patterns they "settle into and continually replicate" within the confines of their enclosures (Bryan-Wilson 2015, 41).

† Describing Serra's short film *Hand Catching Lead* (1969), Krauss acknowledges "its quality of relentless persistence — of doing something over and over again without regarding 'success'" as a particular goal or priority (Krauss 1977, 244). Serra made the film the same year he saw Forti's *Fall-*

ers (see fig. 5), which had no doubt made an impression on him and likely influenced the film (Morse 2016, 154).

‡ While observing animals at the zoo, Forti studied how their bodies were in constant motion. She drew pictures of them eating, walking, rolling, rocking, swaying, and she used these renderings for investigations of "anatomy, ritual movement, gravitational forces, and limberness." These animal drawings demonstrate her attempts to record the extreme pliability of their bodies, to illustrate how the "relationships among their parts" can shift fluidly and rapidly from one gesture to the next (Bryan-Wilson 2015, 35).

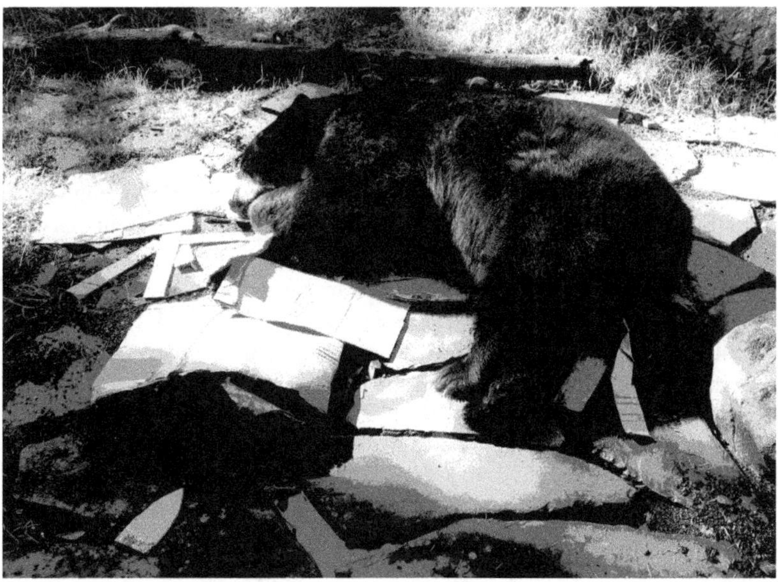

Figure 4. Where do we go when we've no place to be? If captive: unseen. The strange matter of dislocation, isolation.* As a polar bear swings his head, in a dance / state of measure, in communion with forces of which he is part.† This is not a polar bear. I have photographed a black bear in its place. The way negative space makes a shape of absence; we fill in what we want to see. The privilege inherent in this desire. Is this an animal or a sea / of broken-down boxes, a black mass at its center? In our loneliness we devise ways to comfort ourselves, through movement. I am unseen, often. *(But in that place I made him see me.)* We work with what we have. Is this bear taking care of itself, a body at rest‡ or immobilized / in despair? I do not stay long enough to make a determination; just a few hours at the zoo. If we are agents of our own realities, we create opportunities for interaction. Unfortunately, the polar bear habitat is closed for construction. Underscoring the complexities of a liminal space: whether stage, cage, or dance floor. *(Later he emailed, apologetic; he wasn't technically available.)* I'd try to confirm the wording but that account was hacked, shut down years ago.

* Forti was drawn to animals out of "a shared sense of dislocation, loneliness, and isolation" yet attuned "to their moments of connection and collective recreation [...] aware that their movements were shaped not only by their state of captivity but also by their inner reserves of strength" (Bryan-Wilson 2015, 45).

† The topic of measurement was central to much of Forti's thinking and extended into her animal studies. She questioned the arbitrary nature of standardized measurement, how "standard ideals" are determined through "cultural agreement." Connecting these ideas to the processes behind her

pieces, and how they were embodied in animals (including humans), she notes: "It seems to me that when a polar bear swings his head, he is in a dance state. He is in a state of establishing measure, and of communion with the forces of which he is part" (see fig. 9) (Forti 1998, 119).

‡ In multiple texts, Forti describes how she came to identify strongly with the animals she observed and intuited that, as her own movements serve as a marker of her identity to which she can always return, so too can animals retain their specific animal nature. For example, through its inevitably limited movements, a polar bear in captivity was "taking care of itself in a way I could understand. [...] That bear, whose genetic makeup keeps it ranging at great distances over frozen lands, was in a small enclosure in the Rome zoo. Why did my heart identify with its heart? It just did" (Bryan-Wilson 2015, 46).

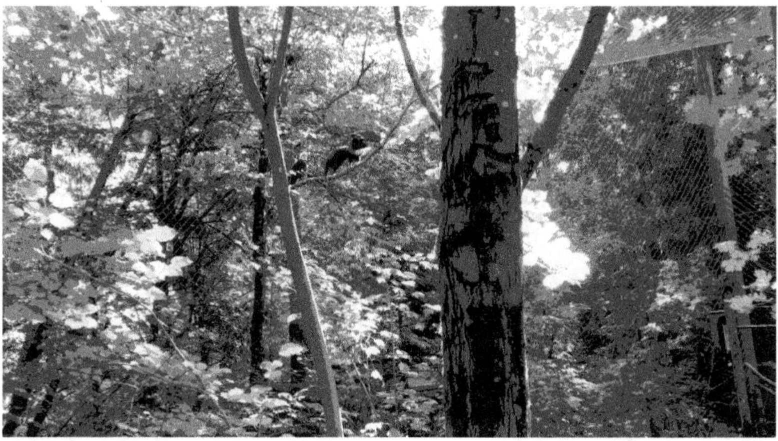

Figure 5. These nets lace the sky: boundaries built to protect us or keep us / confined. Grounded versus allure of flight; or is it falling? I consider cutting this section, but a body subject to gravity seems relevant; I've left it in for now.* So we enter a space / unknown. Strangers wanting to be touched, an interplay made dangerous, thrilling.† So we dance. An act irrational: a measure of / the draw of / falling or. *(When, a year later, I flew cross-country to see him.)* Can you make out the eagles perched on a branch? These birds, of course, can fly but do not have agency here. *(He played Nick Drake on guitar, we watched Fellini.)* If I'm honest, I feel silly describing this scenario, this romance; I deliberately avoid too much specificity. In this essay, I've posterized my images: a system to sidestep revealing what is overly personal. It's hard to be earnest, not trite, in telling a love story. If one can call it that. The goal is not to obfuscate, and yet. The strategy of addressing such material as a technical problem appeals to me.‡

* From the late '60s through the '70s, postmodern dancers' focus on process often involved bodies subject to natural forces: "falling [...] caught up in centrifugal and centripetal forces of Forti's circling; or aligned with the ground" (Morse 2016, 154). Also: how the idea of falling often carries metaphorical meanings, as in *falling for* a ruse, or *falling in love.*

† In Forti's *Fallers* (1968), performers drop from the roof of a seventeenth-floor penthouse to a terrace twelve feet below, providing an "astonishing view of apparent free-fall." The piece presented the body "as the act of falling, and as the fallen," with an intentionally ambiguous degree of agency, making the work appear dangerous and thrilling. Rendering the body as an object, it also "coupled the implicit awareness of the act of *throwing oneself* off a roof with a seemingly heedless absorption in the act of *falling or dropping*" — an irrational act that was "disturbing, disorienting" (Morse 2016, 154).

‡ For postmodern dancers, the notion of integrating material deemed private, of exposing emotion in the work, was complex. They did not eschew its use altogether, but rather, devised ways to allude to the personal in a systematic way. Anna Halprin stated that incorporating the personal "might be best approached as a 'technical problem'" and suggested looking for objective ways to manage such content to make its inclusion possible (quoted in Morse 2016, 21).

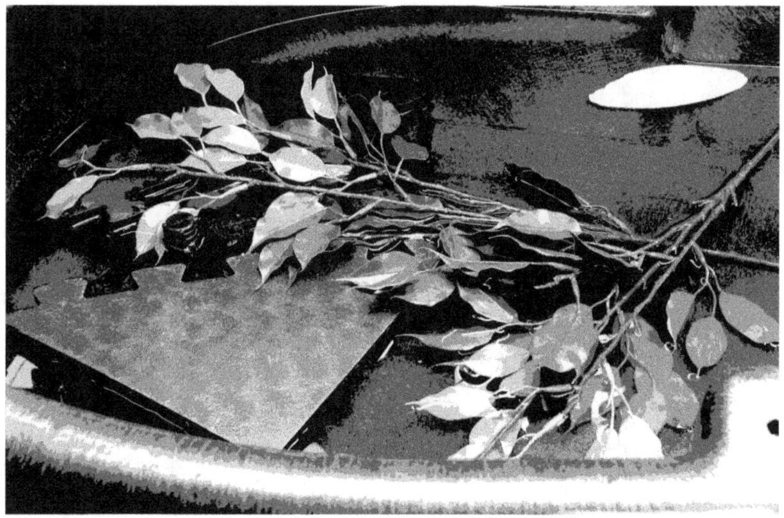

Figure 6. What makes a space of wild abandon?* Do visible walls limit or free us? As I've said, constraints can be generative. I look for hatchlings in a tub of turtles, but they're difficult to see, hidden beneath leaves and some kind of foam. Smaller than a nickel: the perfect size to eat. Human as protector / predator / prey. Watched through glass: small ones, don't get used to people; not a good survival strategy. I make a list of words associated with *club*, another for *zoo*. Look for overlaps. Engineered for unpredictable encounters or. A dance floor as an open field, potentially, ostensibly, for wild abandon.† Rereading the source text, I discover this isn't the salient point; I keep it anyway. How to lower inhibitions, as with alcohol, what a dim light / obscures. Music to overwhelm our senses, making it difficult to hear. *(Yet I was clear in what I wanted, in that space.)*‡ What's acceptable, or encouraged, when boundaries are pushed? Movement as a means / to an end; a mechanism for finding a mate. In dating, I've never much appreciated process, though I wish this weren't true. *(When I learned he was in the area only temporarily, for school.)* But we are all here temporarily. *(What outcome did I need to be satisfied?)*

* Forti's movements based on her animal studies included rolling slowly from one side of a space to another, like seaweed in a surf, and balancing on her hands and toes in a plank position, alternately hopping and then returning to a state of stillness. "More than wild abandon, these small, even modest movements call to mind play as well as entrapment (as in seaweed 'caught' by the waves)" (Bryan-Wilson 2015, 40).

† Forti was interested in the zoo's function as a structural constraint but also as an open field akin to a performance space or stage. She wanted to explore "how dancing bodies — both human and animal — might convey solitude and agitation, but also steadying purpose" (see figs. 4 and 7). Yet

because of the empathy she felt toward the animals, observing them in captivity wore on her; thus many of her works focused on the animals' reserves of strength and their attempts at "self-soothing" (Bryan-Wilson 2015, 45).

‡ In describing what she terms a "dance state" (see fig. 1), Forti refers to an absorption in her movement and an intense awareness of her perceptions, channeled through a "special order of thoughts that come out of the body in motion and which seem to be one with the motion itself." Ironically, she arrives at this sense of heightened awareness through disorientation, brought about, in part, by swinging her head in a dizzying fashion, in the manner of an animal (Morse 2016, 169).

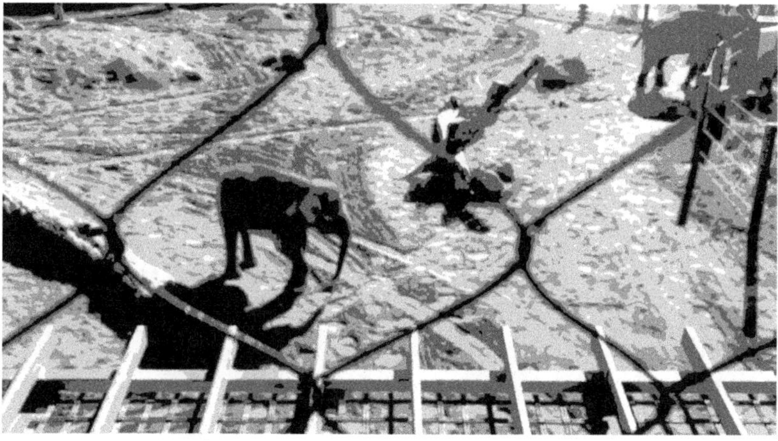

Figure 7. As a zoo is a home is a cage; we are all performers, though the stage and the plot may vary.* Zoom out, see the boundary; zoom in, the fence / disappears. How distance from a subject inevitably alters our perspective. *(How he made me think about sustainability, inadvertent / othering.)* How understanding drives desire / to be better. To be clear, these conversations came about later, post-zoo / I mean, post-dancing. Truth is like a tongue: hard to deny reality once you've tasted it. The nose, of course, also. And don't forget the trunk; how an elephant beats the ground, proving it's safe to walk. Front foot forward, then places the rear one in the same footprint. I've come to watch the elephants dance.† We each have a name, remember. Our muscles oriented in different directions, allowing for greater maneuverability. Imagine: the strength and agility required to balance such a large body.‡

* In addition to observing animals in the zoo, Forti spent a winter in Turin, where she became involved in Michelangelo Pistoletto's collaborative theater troupe Lo Zoo, which performed satirical plays on the streets of fishing villages and elsewhere. The name reflected Pistoletto's belief that "so-called civilization had relegated every animal to its cage. The less dangerous, more docile and submissive had been placed in large common fenced-in areas: factories, housing projects, sport stadiums." Although the piece Forti choreographed for the troupe was never performed, the project is indicative of her close association and identification with animals, reflecting the sense that any creature who lacks agency is essentially captive in a zoo (Bryan-Wilson 2015, 47–48).

† One of Forti's experiences at the Rome zoo that found its way into *Sleepwalkers/Zoo Mantras* was her observation of the movements of an elephant: "I saw an elephant who had perfected a walk with which he passed the time of day. It was a walking backwards and forwards, some four to seven steps each way with, at either end, a slight kick which served to absorb the

momentum and to reverse the direction of travel of that great and finely-balanced bulk." The first sequence in her piece derives from this movement (Forti 1998, 146).

‡ While Forti felt sadness and empathy toward the caged animals she observed, she also viewed them as "models of resourcefulness, of ingenuity, of managing stress, and of endurance" (Bryan-Wilson 2015, 47–48).

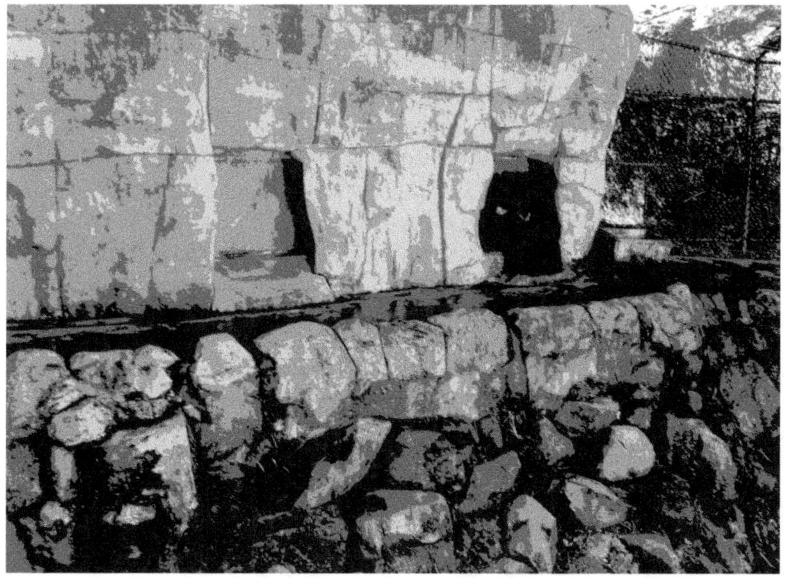

Figure 8. Look carefully for the signs. Stay calm. Slow and quietly back / away don't / run. Allow plenty of room and always identify an escape route. How to behave when encountering a stranger. Look carefully for signs. Make eye contact. Understand a specific gesture, quality of touch. *(Before I left, when he said he didn't want a relationship.)* The desire to connect yet. Hurting is easy or. How to behave when encountering a bear. In this writing, I'd intended to examine different themes in each section; now I reassure myself as they appear to both dissolve and materialize as I go / deeper. *(What could I expect?)* I use the term *relationship* loosely. In these circumstances consider all angles of vulnerability. What if instead of fear* we felt empathy, approached with a presumption of trust rather than malice? In a café an artist recommends exploring grief through the use of dead rats.† *(And did this interaction rate as a failure or success?)* But that isn't the point. I struggle with evaluative measures. How we relate to other bodies, or: intrude on others' spaces. No matter / the animal.‡

* Forti's work showed the potential to bond with others through bodily movement, even across species, as she demonstrated through what she called "passive identification" with the animals at the zoo (Bryan-Wilson 2015, 35). According to one participant in *Huddle* (1961), "You are breathing someone else's breath and you can hear all their sounds [...] you can tell if someone climbing is [...] scared.'" The performers could sense each others' "states of mind through physical cues" (Morse 2016, 147). The vulnerabilities laid bare in this exercise are palpable.

† Focusing significant attention on the anxious behaviors of the animals she studied, Forti's understanding of them was "tinged with grief," as she felt great tenderness and empathy toward them (Bryan-Wilson 2015, 44).

‡ Forti recognized the uneasiness wrought by the zoo "system," which offered examples of "nonverbal exchange, of catalyzing bodily sensations, and of compassion among denigrated subjects." Her dances, in line with the post-humanist thinking of the time, address the constraints fostered by "systems of gender and speciesism, as well as the possibility of surprising alliances across the human/nonhuman divide" (Bryan-Wilson 2015, 49–50).

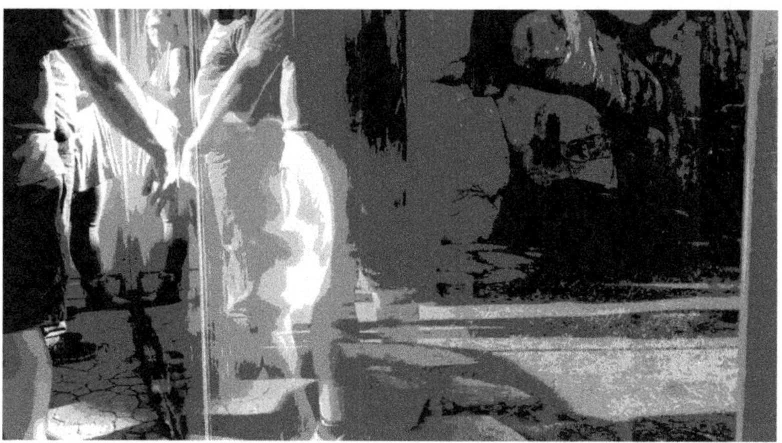

Figure 9. How our bodies know to move yet / we ape lions, bears.* A man's hand taps the glass inches from her head. Taunting, luring. The sun's reflection makes it difficult to discern the subject and its actions. So much depends on / context, the configuration of boundaries. I search for reason. The lion's walk along a wall: a means of self-soothing or: plotting against unsuspecting prey. The latter does not align nicely with an empathetic stance. A way of maintaining / control or simply what we want to see. Desire, by definition, is irrational. *(Our story didn't have a lot of plot points.)* I almost forget to mention him here. *(We stayed in touch a while, I'd see him when he visited.)* I still haven't adequately addressed the notion of dating as process. Alas. How this essay loops back to the beginning, the closest I come to mimicking patterns of postmodern dancers. How I tried, failed to use a series of overlapping circles, triangles.† As a lion retraces a path along glass, enacting the ongoing nature of things. How tomorrow, the activities of today could be forgotten, as if they never occurred. Or rather, simply continued as a series of repetitions, evolving variations, with no apparent beginning / end.

* Among Forti's zoo subjects were large cats, in whom she observed adaptability and strength. In her writing, she discusses their compulsive pacing along the border of their enclosures, which seemed to provide some degree of relief and offered her a new sense of what she was doing when she danced. Movement is, for the animals as well as for her, a method of control and redirected awareness: "At times I've escaped an oppressive sense of fragmentation by plunging my consciousness into cyclical momentum" (Bryan-Wilson 2015, 45–46).

† The emphasis on patterning in process art and 1970s dance manifested in many ways — from drawn vocal scores to repeated sequences of simple gestures to a focus on spatial structures, which included mapping out how movements would be performed across a space. These techniques enabled

artists to explore the same materials and concepts in new ways. For example, Lucinda Childs's *Particular Reel* (1973) features a series of circular revolutions, a repeated phrase that makes an "unbroken loop" (Morse 2016, 159–60). For her part, Forti often worked with numerical patterns and connected them with movement subject to gravitational forces: "I use the numerals as a floor pattern but I try to move through the curves and straight lines as dynamically as possible. In that way my sense of the figures is really kinesthetic; I work with the centrifugal and other forces with a sense of measure." For a section of *Home Base* (1979), she created a floor plan with seven circles and two intersecting triangles, Arabic numerals contained within them. Accompanied by drawings with clustered circles representing the Star of David overlaid with the numerals, this floor plan would guide her pattern of movements on the dance floor (Morse 2016, 163).

Notes

In Figure 4, the line "Unfortunately, the polar bear habitat is closed for construction" was taken from the home page of the Oregon Zoo website while the area was under renovation (*Oregon Zoo* n.d.; the notice cited here is no longer available).

In Figure 6, the lines "I look for the hatchlings but they are so hard to see, hidden beneath leaves and foam. Smaller than a nickel. The perfect size to eat" are adapted from a page from the Oregon Zoo website (*Oregon Zoo* 2018).

In Figure 7, the lines relating to an elephant's trunk as a steadying instrument and descriptions of the muscles of the tongue and nose are adapted from Pomeroy (2013) and the Elephant Nature Park website (*Elephant Nature Park* n.d.).

The instructions at the beginning of Figure 8 are from signs at the Oregon Zoo.

STAGE → PAGE

The ideas of process art — an emphasis on structures and geometric forms, repetition and reversal, and examination of the methods and materials with which art is made — heavily informed the approaches of Forti, Rainer, and their contemporaries. Influenced by and at times pushing against early mentors, especially Halprin, Cunningham, Dunn, and Cage, they and their postmodern contemporaries have employed a variety of overlapping techniques, including collage, chance procedures, collaboration, and improvisation, which allow them to subvert habit and avoid predictable outcomes.

Both Forti and Rainer have incorporated chance procedures into their work at times over the years, although they resist strict adherence to this technique. In her *News Animations,* Forti translates and animates the news of the day through spontaneous movement and speech. With her fragmented and associational approach, she makes meaning and offers glimpses of narrative, counter to the chance-based process of Cage and other postmodernists. And Rainer has made clear from the beginning that she resists the notion of chance dominating the compositional process. Speaking of a pivotal workshop she and Forti took with Dunn, she said, "[Chance] seemed to be the end-all. If you made it by chance, then anything was okay" (Morse 2016, 45).

In a conversation about her dance *The Concept of Dust, or How Do You Look When There's Nothing Left to Move?* Rainer notes that she continues to use a collage method she learned from Cunningham: "[T]he feet are doing one thing and the body is doing something else, not related, and so we start patching stuff together" (Rainer 2015a). In that same conversation, she explains her use of improvisation and collaboration: "[A]side from the particular movements, when and where and who does them and where they take place is entirely up to the performers. So it means it's different at every performance."

Likely due in part to having less technical training than many of her peers, Forti appears to have more fully embraced improvisation "as a means to find new and unprecedented ways of moving" (Burt 2006, 14). Much of this originated in her work with Halprin, whose approach involved following a stream of consciousness:

> We worked at achieving a state of receptivity in which the stream of consciousness could spill out unhampered. But at the same time a part of the self acted as a witness, watching for movement that was fresh and good, watching the whole of what was evolving between us. At times after a session, I had the feeling that even if I died that night, as one might die any night, the improvisation had grounded itself, and had become an autonomous moment of communion. (Forti 1998, 32)

Forti recalls her early days studying improvisation with Halprin, and thinking, "No, that makes sense in terms of the movement. No, that makes sense in terms of a repetition of something. No, that makes sense. It's an obvious association. Oh my god, where did that come from? I'll use that." Cunningham and Cage would say that resisting one's natural impulses in art-making is essentially impossible to do, because while improvising, one inevitably resorts to old habits. "But we were using our own mind to find something that was not an old habit" (Forti 2015).

It was through this work with Halprin that Forti first discovered the sensitivity that she wanted dancers and audiences to observe in the qualities of movement that emerged in her dance constructions, such as *See-Saw,* originally performed in collaboration with Rainer and Bob Morris (Burt 2006, 59). As Rainer explains, the piece involved a sequence of unrelated events, and its improvisational nature both inspired and thrilled her:

> At one point Bob Morris read *Art News* to himself, and I had my first screaming fit on the other end. That came about through Simone flinging a ragged jacket on the floor and saying, 'Improvise that!' and I went to town on my end of the see-saw, screaming and yelling. I couldn't wait. [...] What impressed me structurally about it was that she made no effort to connect the events thematically in any way. I mean the see-saw and the two people, that was the connecting tissue. And one thing followed another. Whenever I'm in doubt, I think of that. One thing following another. (Burt 2006, 59–60)

Forti's practice of improvisation, which often combines movement and words, is now part of her legacy, as she has throughout her career worked to erase barriers between art forms, as well as between the body and mind:

> Movement, or improvisation, always involves following impulses while also watching the whole situation. [...] There is always thinking going on while the movement is happening. [...] What I want to impart [...] is the experience of having the motor centers and the verbal centers of your mind communicating with one another, working together. I want to facilitate that dialogue. (Perron 2021)

We likewise wanted to foreground process and employ the above-mentioned methodologies, including a similarly flexible approach to chance operations. As with our first book, this is a collaboration, although differently configured: We worked together closely to develop the concept and procedure for generating the essays, which we then wrote separately. The initial process, described in greater detail in the "Surprising Leaps" section later in the book, blended chance, collage, and improvisation. Once we began writing, we continued to employ these elements in a variety of ways, each experimenting with how far we could approach Rainer and Forti's performance-oriented work while simultaneously recognizing that writing produces a permanent artifact necessitating a different mode of engagement than live performance, for both creator and audience.

The Five Positions: Assaying the Personal in Postmodern Art

Sarah Rosenthal

1.

This is a five paragraph essay about the five positions • This essay will explain something • in particular how dancer-choreographer Simone Forti inserted the personal in her work but filtered so it came across as a ghost-like trace • and why • and how this resonates with a person with a history • and doesn't • It's complicated • as they say in the dating profiles these days • but not complicated as in relationships • although fundamentally you could say so much is about relationships • Take attachment theory • John Bowlby • Mary Ainsworth • Mary Main • their gang • their gang's explanation of how a person is formed • The way the parent makes or fails to make themself available to the infant affects how the infant is attached • e.g., insecurely securely and so forth • And that shapes their whole life • Even if they do a lot of healing they are marked by that profound experience • I think Simone Forti was securely attached • She speaks glowingly of her parents • her childhood • She even forgives her father for being patriarchal • She claims it worked out because her mother had her own sphere of influence • the household • And her father said Simone could do whatever she wanted • She does • always has • more than most people • She's a *conceptualist* • a word that scares me • But her concepts are anchored in her body • She never leaves her body • She learned about kinesthetic awareness • the awareness of one's body as it moves through space • in the 1950s from Anna Halprin at the latter's open-air studio in the Bay Area at the base of Mount Tam • Forti and her husband Robert Morris dropped out of Reed • It is a sign of privilege • to feel safe dropping out of an excellent school • to know they'd be able to make their way • to the Bay • where they found Halprin • You could say Forti imprinted on Halprin • As long as I've raised attachment theory • *imprinting* is a term proposed by Konrad Lorenz • The Father of Modern Ethology • whom Bowlby, Ainsworth, and Main considered their forerunner • Lorenz used the term to describe how the first creature whom baby geese see becomes their mother • even if it's Konrad Lorenz • They will follow that creature to the ends of the earth • But Forti is not a goose • Forti was deeply influenced by Halprin but later pushed away •

like a teenager rebelling • as she put it "pushing mommy away" • When Forti did that she was not biologically a teenager • but art has its own arc • From Halprin • Forti learned the term "kinesthetic awareness" • and even though so much happened in her life • Multiple marriages • Robert Morris • Bob Whitman • Peter Van Riper • multiple locations • Italy which her family left when she was four to escape Mussolini and where she returned for a time in her 20s • the aforementioned Reed • the aforementioned Bay Area • New York • hippy commune existence in the Woodstock area after Woodstock • Vermont • Los Angeles • multiple art forms • dance • drawing • writing • singing • performance art • sculpture • she never lost track of kinesthetic awareness • Kinesthetic awareness was her basis • always • I try to feel my feet on the earth • when I walk from here to there • I try to tune into my center • Forti does • That's probably what allows her to have these diverse experiences • and not get chewed up • Some of that 1969–1970 Woodstock period sounds pretty dicey • Hand-to-mouth and quasi-homeless • But Forti is always home • She feels safe in the world • A sense of safety I attribute partly to privilege • She would agree • "I really have had a lot of privilege" • Yet my gut says there's still value in what her sense of safety allows her to explore • Although as a woman it seems from the outside like she's been screwed in ways • she refutes • Some interviewers sound uncomfortable on her behalf • politely pointing out how she gave up her art to support Whitman's for several years • But she doesn't frame it that way • "I'm not so against paternalism" • What can anyone say • She's Forti • Not just a person or persona but a personage • at this point • for those who are into her work • like me •

2.

A lot of the edgier '60s art challenged the traditional notion of self • John Cage the Buddhist influenced multiple genres • For a long time art historians focused more on the influence of Marcel Duchamp on these young artists • his concept of the readymade • But more recently Cage emerges • in the foreground • Forti's first mentor was Halprin • from whom she learned kinesthetic awareness plus improvisation and a task-like approach • Then she pushed mommy away • as she put it • But note how profound the word mommy • You can push all you want but you've been imprinted • She moved with Morris to New York • where she got into Cage's concepts via Robert Dunn • learned to create procedures • that generate a piece of art • but kept the beating heart • of Halprin • No one quite knew how to deal with her work's powerful affective dimension • for example folk songs and various vocalizations • so they kind of just ignored that part • focused on aspects that aligned with more acceptable • at that time • elements • like Minimalism • Only more recently • for example with the publication of Meredith Morse's book *Soft Is Fast* • is the intense affect • these ghostlike traces of the personal • in Forti's work • celebrated • Part of me can really relate to the ghost-remainder approach • It so accords with what I learned from my graduate school poetry writing teacher • She'd speak in quiet tones • of work by • for example • Paul Celan • whose poetry • can be seen as an oblique daily journal • of his encounters • with traumatic memory • and its ongoing grip on his existence • A question I ask daily is • How can you use traumatic memory • and not be used by it • This is something artists • who traffic in trauma • must do • must learn how to do • Interestingly Forti and Celan were both marked by anti-Semitism • Forti's family having escaped Mussolini when she was four • but Forti overall led a much more protected life • as mentioned • Sometimes the traumatic traces • in her pieces • have more to do with things like breakups • For example one of what she called • her "elevation tunes" • where she created a musical score • using all her vertical locations • a building's sixth floor • the subway and so on • over two weeks • as notes • to be whistled by her friend • composer La Monte

Young • It just so happens • during this two weeks • she was sick in bed a lot • ending a relationship with Morris • starting one with Whitman • A lot going on • And it so happens • the next time she made such a tune • was five years later • on the verge of breaking up with Whitman • These aren't traumas on the order of what Celan experienced • losing his parents to the Nazis • forced to haul stones in a camp • displaced • And some of Forti's ghostlike traces aren't traumatic at all • like "Face Tunes" • melodies derived from outlines of people's faces • Yet Forti and Celan and so many others shared this aesthetic • It was in the air • a sense of being sickened by the small self following its predictable myopic narrative arc • like the caged animals • Forti communes with • in her "Zoo Mantras" • She paces • pads • and swings • We were meant for wide-open spaces • We survive our conditions as best we can • until we can't • Dear reader • do you wonder • what all this has to do with the five positions • Do you think of ballet • how it is based on the five positions • "the" • as if there are only five • positions • the body must learn to hold • What other associations do you have • Do you love to watch ballet dancers twirl and leap • arch and split • Do you love dying swans • secretly strong as oxes • lifted by muscled men • Do you stumble across information about grueling routines • Brutal competition • "You test them," Mr. Martins said • "What are they made of? Am I wrong, am I right? You throw little bones to them and see how they react" • Do you think of foot bones • encased in their little torture chambers • Is this old news • Or maybe you never bought the fantasy • I did •

3.

Kinesthetic awareness • guided Forti's every move • When she relocated to New York she signed up for classes with Martha Graham and Merce Cunningham • but couldn't and wouldn't • suck in her tummy like Graham • couldn't and wouldn't • grasp the lightning-fast motions of Cunningham's feet • For all of these two giants' success in moving dance past the tired balletic body • They imposed their own physical constraints • constraints • Forti refused • So what a breath of fresh air • Dunn's workshop • where an adventurous set of young dancers and artists • came together to do task-based exercises • based on chance operations and time structures and scores • an approach Dunn had learned from Cage • who got the idea of chance operations from throwing the Yijing • Many assume the use of chance involves relinquishing control of outcomes • But Forti points out that's not true • Rather • you're choosing • "the distance between the point of control and the final movement performed" • She became interested in taking • as she says • "precise readings of what points of control I was using, and wanted to use, and to what effect" • Kinesthetically speaking • whenever I read that sentence • the rigorous logic of it • the core of me from throat to abdomen • tightens • A wave of nausea • washes over me • A cold heat • spreads down my arms • Just last week I learned the term "affective filter" • Stephen Krashen • a bilingual education advocate • invented it to describe what can happen to multilanguage learners • A screen descends between them and the words they want to learn • The screen might include anxiety • low self-confidence • low motivation • When I saw this term I thought • That term explains what happens when I read or try to think about certain kinds of matter • for example the notion of making conceptual art • when making art becomes a matter of solving for X • and if you get it wrong • the reader will scratch their head • or worse • scrawl a bad grade on your paper • I was a gender of my generation • good at math till I hit adolescence • Had grown up taking ballet classes from Dinah Cody • She'd been a real ballerina • Had a corner on the market in my neighborhood • The older girls got to go *en pointe* • Who didn't want to • be a dying swan • Some didn't • But I • still wanted that in the interval during which I entered my teens • just before I went to the alternative high school • and embraced second wave feminism • I signed up at a real ballet school • downtown • Must have been on Wabash • Near the Capezio store • where you bought your regulation black leotard • regulation pale pink tights • regulation pink slippers • regulation pink toe shoes • These • you were told to clomp around in • break them in • while getting used to the whole idea • of going *en pointe* • although being restricted to clomping • reinforced the point that you were still an ugly duckling • First you needed to master • the five positions • and various routines based on them • We stood at the barre • A trim and grim maestro with a European accent • I forget which • maybe Russian • maybe French • called out terse orders • The girls complied • My affective filter descended • thick with messages • You are ugly • You are awkward • You have the wrong body • The wrong mind • You will never master the routines • barked by the strict man • Believe it or not • That wasn't the trauma • The trauma was an event too good to be true • in the sense that the symbolism of it • now looking back • points to what's wrong with ballet classes for adolescent girls • and in a larger sense • the whole ballet machine • the worldview it's based on • but at the time • the symbolism pointed to • what was wrong with me • I can't categorize the trauma • It wasn't genocide • or the experience of multilanguage learners many of whom cross the border out of desperation or necessity • It wasn't a breakup • Or an illness • though some were still framing it that way •

4.

Of her piece "Face Tunes" Forti writes • "I've never let the audience know they were listening to patterns derived from faces" • "I had faith that, since the awareness of variations among similar events is so basic a life process" • "when they heard 'Face Tunes' • they would unconsciously sense a familiar kind of order." • I can relate to that • It reminds me of the aforementioned poetry teacher • quoting Celan • and so many others • She too resisted the tired trope • of confession • She'd been influenced by the Language poets • who • like Forti and her ilk • reacted against the petty bourgeois self • that dominated art mid-century and later • keeping us distracted from inconveniences like Vietnam • These young artists coming up in the '60s and '70s • were ripping the scales off our eyes • The self is a lie • served up by late capitalism • to get you to buy • the notion that you're a "consumer" • not a "citizen" • It's a bill of goods • I got it • How liberating • to be relieved of the burden of self • Besides I was going to meditation retreats • I'm not a Buddhist but I act like one • Self is a construction • Anyone can know that • So Forti's approach makes all kinds of sense to me • to the small self • rather • that is trying to communicate in language • a kind of prose • which makes avoidance of the terms *I* and *my* and *me* difficult • But that's OK • We all know language is an imperfect vehicle • But another part • of this small self • clings to the personal narrative • the narrative arc • Maybe I read too much Plath • in my adolescence • Panzer-man and all that • In 1976 • a few years after I attended that ballet class • my parents attended a concert • on Michigan Avenue • They came home bemused • describing a piece by Cage • a Native American alone on a stage banging a drum • as white audience members gathered their furs and purses and streamed out • My parents were hip enough to stay • They didn't get it • but they sensed something interesting going on • It must have been "Apartment House 1776" • representing the four religious traditions practiced at the US's founding • The piece included • a voice solo by Swift Eagle • from the Apache and Santo Domingo Pueblo tribes • and there were drums involved • Either my parents' description or my memory is muddy • But I think this was the piece • By then I'd abandoned ballet • I was enamored of modern dance • which was already over as far as Cage, Forti, and their crowd were concerned • Cunningham • Cage's partner • being The Father of Postmodern Dance • But modern was and still is going strong • As is ballet for that matter • Girls still sign up to deform their feet • get thrown bones • by the likes of Peter Martins • My parents' bemused openness to art they didn't understand • their willingness to hang in there while droves of season ticket holders stomped angrily past them out into the night • made a big impression • you could say imprinted me • primed me for that LangPo-inflected approach to poetry • So why can't I relinquish the personal entirely • Why these I's and my's and me's • infiltrating this piece • like signals of a diagnosis • Narcissistic Personality Disorder • Well • besides that poetry teacher • my other main graduate school instructor • was a founder of New Narrative • a prose form developed to represent selves and stories • primarily queer and working class but inclusive of other marginalities too • that had been excluded from the master narrative • influenced by Language poetry • LangPo as it's referred to • derisively • affectionately • or just economically • but rejecting the latter's purist stance regarding the "I" • the "my" • the "me" • claiming story • but telling it slant • Not blinded by the construct of self • but inhabiting self • in a slippery way • That made as much sense to me • as my poetry teacher's rejection of pronouns • though given the aforementioned • affective filter • which made it hard to read or write freely • I could only intermittently execute either model •

5.

Forti does not consider herself a feminist • She says things like • "I'm not so against paternalism" • Regardless • reducing the personal to a ghostlike trace • creates space for women • who have been trapped by the narrative of ballet • For that matter • the way she and others blew apart genre distinctions • also created a space • where no one knew what was what • which arguably made it easier for women to step in • and make dances • or whatever you want to call them • Forti's own work • operates at a juncture between many forms • Most often she's called something like • "dancer-choreographer" • a shorthand • inadequate as pronouns • to describe the flux and flow of reality Forti works with • a project • impossible to do justice to here • But to give you just a taste • here's part of her description of a piece called *Day Night* • "Some years ago, a few hours before having to perform, I was afraid that I had forgotten how to dance" • "I couldn't imagine dancing" • "I was standing outside the performance hall when, crouching slightly" • "I set my right foot forward and opened my hands to my sides" • "'Is this how?' I asked myself" • "I begin 'Day Night' with this movement" • Forti's work is deeply personal • But she doesn't broadcast it • She prefers for the audience to feel the ghostlike traces • Her work is informed • by rigorous concepts • that cause an affective filter • to clamp down on my mind • But I realize • this is one of those "aha moments" • her concepts • are grounded in kinesthetic awareness • Her ideas • rise up out of her body • don't block it like a steel screen rising up blocking her from life • I realize • I'm avoiding saying why I developed this affective filter in the first place • a filter filled with messages • like • You are ugly • You are lazy • You are clumsy • You are stupid • If you can't do it right the first time don't do it at all • Unhelpful messages like that • It's another thing I just can't do justice to here • Dear reader • you're going to have to trust me on this one • I can give a smattering • For example my father's family were Jews who fled Nazi Germany • except for all the ones who didn't make it out • But that doesn't really explain • why he abused his children • nor • why my mom tolerated it • We all know lots of families propel and propound such abuse • generation after generation • It's a larger cultural story • a true story • the small self gets trapped in • adolescence is tough enough • without being told what a failure you are • as a daughter • thinker • doer • human • I tried to escape through various means • Engaged in a lot of magical thinking • one example of which was my short stint in classical ballet • "Ballet will reshape my body" • "I will become a graceful swan" • A few classes into my new plan • during a *demi-plié* • I glanced down • to see • two ruby half moons on my inner thighs • where regulation pink tights • met regulation black crotch • In a panic • I motioned to the accompanist • who • as you might expect • wore a beehive • cat glasses • a cigarette holder • Speech • unless you were the maestro • was verboten • So was leaving • But the cat-eyed beehived accompanist motioned me out the door • I ran • to the dressing room • The older girls • lounged leggily on benches • or did limbering stretches • *en pointe* • One I knew vaguely • I asked her for a pad • She only had • a tampon • which in those days • created pain localized yet radiating • I felt faint • another item on the long long list of things that seemed wrong with me • I doubt I returned to that class • But my memory • may be blotted • by two bloody half moons • which • looking back • seem the perfect symbol • for what's wrong with traditional ballet • its diminishment of female sexuality • such that the appearance of menstrual blood • would cause such pure shame • Looking back • those ruby moons seem beautiful • spreading larger by the second • a process • Forti might celebrate • given her commitment to the flow • of time • the nature • of the animal body • yours • dear reader • and mine • not mediated • here • right now •

Notes

Paragraph 1:

Some of the material in this section was informed by Forti (1998) and Morse (2016).

"pushing mommy away," "I really have had a lot of privilege," and "I'm not so against paternalism" are from Forti (2010).

"kinesthetic awareness"' is from Morse (2016, 4).

Paragraph 2:

"'ghost remainder"' is from Morse (2016, 119).

Some of the material in this section was informed by "Simone Forti Goes to the Zoo," by Julia Bryan-Wilson, in *October Magazine, Ltd.*

"You test them ..." is from Cooper (2017).

Paragraph 3:

"the distance between ..." and "precise readings ..." are from Morse (2016, 50).

For a description of Stephen Krashen's affective filter theory, see Krashen (2009).

Paragraph 4:

"I've never let ..." and "I had faith ..." are from Morse (2016, 116).

For a description of "Apartment House 1776," see Wikipedia, s.v. "Apartment House 1776," https://en.wikipedia.org/wiki/Apartment_House_1776.

Paragraph 5:

Forti prefers the term *movement artist* to describe her work.

"Some years ago ..." is from Forti (1998, 144).

SURPRISING LEAPS

As we began thinking through the potential contours of this project, we discovered an interview with Simone Forti by Alessandra Nicifero for the Robert Rauschenberg Foundation (2015). Forti proposed that Nicifero develop a process incorporating the element of chance into the conversation. In response Nicifero created a grid of associations that included significant locations based on Forti's travels, time periods of Forti's life, key figures in Forti's world, and themes related to movement and actions relevant to Forti's work; by rolling dice, they determined the category of discussion and one other specific element. We borrowed both the grid and the notion of a chance-oriented process to generate a set of intersections of our personal experiences and artistic themes that emerged from our research on Forti and Rainer; each of these intersections became the focal point of an essay.

In addition, in the spirit of linking the work of these dancer-choreographers and our own associations with dance, we sought to literally embody the broader topic of our book by incorporating movement into our process. Gestures we generated to accompany five dance-related memories became part of the process by which we developed associations in each essay between a memory and theme.

In this way, we allowed chance and dance to guide the focus of each essay.

- **The themes:** We each identified five recurring themes in Rainer and Forti's work, for a total of ten themes, and numbered them 1–10.
- **The memories:** We each identified five personal memories related to dance and numbered them 1–5.
- **The gestures:** We each created a gesture or movement representing each of the five dance-related memories.
- **The grid:** We each created a large grid, ten squares by five squares — Valerie on her back patio, Sarah on her living room floor — which would enable us to randomly pair the ten themes with our five respective memories. (See the following grid.)

	Memory 1	Memory 2	Memory 3	Memory 4	Memory 5
Theme 1					
Theme 2					
Theme 3					
Theme 4					
Theme 5					
Theme 6					
Theme 7					
Theme 8					
Theme 9					
Theme 10					

The process for pairing themes and memories:

1. Each of us wrote the numbers 1–5 on slips of paper and placed them in a jar.
2. We each selected a number randomly and, once all five numbers were pulled, gave the sequence to the other.
3. The recipient of the numbers set a timer for five minutes, then improvised a dance grounded in the memory and gesture tied to the first number, within the confines of the grid.
4. When the timer went off, she froze and took note of her point of contact with the grid.
5. The dancer then sent the grid coordinates nearest the point of contact to the other person.
6. We repeated the process until we had each sent and received five sets of coordinates.
7. After receiving the coordinates, we each wrote essays that addressed the paired themes and memories as represented by the coordinates.

We found that some of the randomly generated combinations corresponded naturally in terms of topics and tone, whereas others at first seemed quite a stretch. But Rainer and Forti's work illustrates how such leaps can generate compelling work. So in our writing, we welcomed the sometimes-awkward juxtapositions — the thrilling "Oh my god, where did that come from?" moments — created through our chance-based process.

Listening through the Body: An Exercise in Sustained Coordination

Valerie Witte

To strike *shime-daiko* (*shime* for short) / two
heads held together, fastened by cords / we
raise, drop to skins taut across / *bachi* made
of magnolia or some other wood / pitch high
as a god might command a small body
bound / so it's easy to follow
the *ji* (short for *jiuchi*) / align time, tuned
in to calibrate beats / to make
an ensemble / dynamically
listen.

Do

Watching the Taiko Sisters perform at the Cole Valley Street Fair in San Francisco, I think: I want to do that. *To re-engage in music — a discipline I'd long dabbled in but to which I'd sadly lost all connection, in a participatory sense. To again immerse myself in Japanese culture, to which I've been drawn since childhood, when I'd bonded, through origami-folding and letter-writing, with the exchange students my brother befriended in college. To develop the level of focus required to stay attuned to the presence and playing of all members of an ensemble, in sync in movement, sound. To experience the pure appeal — the thrill — of hitting something very hard. This is how I decide to learn taiko drumming. A reach for me? Definitely. But sometimes you need something to climb.*

Ko

Simone Forti's *Huddle* (1961): A group of people stand facing each other, huddled. Together a cluster of limbs, torsos, heads, "a sculpture made of bodies." Take turns climbing — one at a time up this "single structural entity," feet, hands, knees finding surfaces — thighs, shoulders — to support their weight as they maneuver up and over, spontaneously, opportunistically. Move across, down the other side, before "rejoining the mass." No planned sequence of who will climb. Yet knowing when someone has decided to be next. Operating in silence, intuiting when one is preparing to ascend, each member adjusting position and balance accordingly.

Do

Taiko Sisters do not accept beginners. A year and a half after the performance, I coordinate, finally, with the director of Maikaze Daiko *(dancing wind) to sign up for classes. The name is apt; founder Bruce "Mui" Ghent is a taiko master with a degree in modern dance and choreography. In his compositions, qualities of theatricality, meditativeness, and grace — notable in a form often characterized by power — feature prominently. Works exploring social issues and historically significant — often sobering — events. Yet for me the most challenging element? The prevalence of dance, which I find utterly terrifying — and exhilarating.*

Ko

What the body could do, any measure of movement. Anna Halprin, with whom Forti had studied, viewed different positions as problems to solve. What the body would give, to discover the range of responses possible when driven beyond habit or plan. Build awareness "of the sensations in your body," the "changing dynamic configurations." But more than that. To wake from sleep with a sense of a dream landscape — in memory but also in limbs. Observe movement in nature — a tree or water, ants on a hill — take it into the body, abstracted. A step off a curb, the fall of a leaf, every gesture possessing its own quality. Expanding one's movement vocabulary. The more one explored, the more material could be generated, articulated. And in each new movement, a "welcome surprise."

Do

Rudimentary improvisation or an exercise in gauging connection, version one: "Ann had us walk together in a circle, not single-file, but simply all moving in the same direction around a general circular path. [...] We started out very slow, and over a period of an hour gradually picked up more and more speed until we were running. We ran for some time and then started to slow down. The slowing-down process was much faster than the speeding-up process. Within this general speeding up, running and slowing down there were several minor speed-ups and slow-downs. We finally came to a stop and collapsed on the ground."

Ko

When Sensei grows frustrated with my self-proclaimed inability to execute a dance movement, he demands that I apply my "kinesthetic intelligence" to the task at hand. My immediate response: I don't have any. Even a supposedly simple turn or jump is by no means simple for me. Occasionally, we explore techniques used by dancers: When spinning, focus on a point in the room, moving your head and body to visually locate the spot. Giving a sense of stability while the world swirls around. To ignore the signal from the inner ear that cues the sensation of spinning — a convenient rewiring of the brain. This a small glimpse into a world foreign to me, surfacing a notion: Could dance be taught — even, potentially, to me?

II

Let's begin to arrange / ourselves as one
formation in concert / what's a requiem
if not for / communion / interjection
of voice, don't forget breath, centering / where
players, our parts interweave / think of ways
to sustain / rhythm / don't think too much, just
respond / beyond measure / within
listening to the body or how
the body / listens / sound
is movement too.

Do

Let's begin with the warmup. Ritualized, routinized exercises to transition from outside to the realm of taiko. Stretching, counting together — these are ways to move and think in sync. To "experience a place [...] in which Japanese-based customs and training fuse with contemporary Western physical training [where] taiko is integrated into our bodies." Of ki *or spirit: to connect drilling and building a relationship between player and drum. Through sound and energy, create a sense of oneness with the taiko, other members, and ultimately, the audience.*

Ko

I practice (sort of) the introductory sequence of "Requiem dei Tambori." (Do I need to be able to do this if I'll be out of town for the performance? Can I?) Each running out into "aisles" created by a series of chū-daiko *(medium-sized drums) situated high on stands, arranged on a diagonal. So that, looking at the stage, the audience can see us all, staggered. This a mostly somber, meditative piece, somewhat quiet for extended periods but for an audio recording featuring an electronic tone resembling a drone. Periodic interjections of a live score: percussion, singing. In theory, after charging past the drums, we spin, leap back to them one by one — quickly cross into, out of each other's paths — then strike. An interplay of movement and stillness, silence and sound.*

Ko

In ballet and modern dance, performers are conventionally silent, truths of human experience communicated through movement only. Forti's work with voice was, however — suffused with kinesthetic awareness, yes, but also with the qualities, complexities of sound. She was informed by Halprin's approach plus a curiosity, an inclination to explore sustained, unusual vocalization and by experimental music and conceptual word pieces of composers like La Monte Young, with whom she worked at Halprin's San Francisco Dancer's Workshop.

Don

In Young's "Lecture 1960," a reframing: a way to "get inside a sound," experienced on its own terms rather than forced into an "acceptable" form. What's required: prolonged exposure to held tones, listening closely to the harmonics within a note. Listening itself a central act — impressed upon the body in a moment of engagement. The observer is called to attune not just her ears but her whole body, to respond in ways outside the usual sensory framework. For Forti such immersion represents a "bodily relation to space, expressed vocally, that could be shared with participants or onlookers." The body rendered "coextensive" with space, or becoming "cavernous, a resonant chamber."

Ko

What does Requiem *require? Alertness, attention to all the movement onstage — performers weaving around drums, one another. We take care to avoid collision. Tempo, volume vary greatly from one section to the next. A running start; later, a slow walk. A coffin carried, comfort offered. Then taken away. Each of us enacts our own gesture indicating grief. Sensei's voice rising in that space, in song, in a tongue we do not understand. What matter? A mournfulness conveyed unless, until. Clamor of drums, percussion, an urgency in movement.*

Do

Forti's *See-Saw* (1960): Two people on opposite sides of a seesaw, "listening" to each other, any movement or adjustment by one directly affecting the position of the other. In the debut, Yvonne Rainer and Robert Morris vocalized in tandem, in accordance with the movement of the apparatus. At one point Rainer screamed while Morris read in monotone from a magazine. These audio elements were largely improvisational, requiring close attention to remain connected, literally, in balance. Toward the end, Forti sang a song while the see-sawers shifted carefully back and forth on their knees.

II

Don / we strike to the right (♩) / mouth writing
mnemonic, *kuchi-shōga:* we sing to verbalize
patterns to play / a kind of vocabulary / *Do Ko* notated
right-left to the head (two ♩) / a syllable for every
tradition / each corresponding, tongue to drum
shime, chū-daiko / each mouth its own
chatter / how we learn sticking, mark timbre
and time / *Ka* right to the rim (♩) / *Ka Ra* / right /
left to the rim (two ♩) / each drumbeat
vocalized.

Ko

Forti's *Platforms* (1961): A male and a female performer lie underneath two wooden boxes, whistling a tune. Listening. In a relaxed state of easy communion. Each inhalation silent, the same duration as normal breathing. Boxes "as resonating chambers," the sound "clear and penetrating." How silence prompts reflection, draws attention while allowing elements of an environment to seep in, for "a work to be seen *through*." No time frame allotted, pitch to hit, melody to perform, tempo to adhere to, or series of steps to follow. Just two in sync, attuned to the sounds their partner makes. A kind of conversation. Scoreless, continuous physical adjustment to a dynamic situation. Rendered contiguous the spaces of the performers' bodies, their sonorous inner cavities, the wooden boxes reverberating with noises of their inhabitants — and in relation to the space in which the figures lie.

Do

How do we locate the center? Slow walk around, then find ourselves behind drums, bending. Five chū-daiko *arranged in a line, skirted to the floor. What goes on underneath, obstructed. Players, too, obscured from the audience. Suddenly spring up, to the side, in unison striking:* Do Ko. *(Rest, rest.)* Do Ko. *(Rest, rest.) This is how we've learned. A phonetic sound for each stroke indicates duration, placement on the drum. Are we speaking or listening?* Do Ko Do Ko Ko Don Ko Do Ko. *Each set preceded by a "reach," arms outstretched for more power, more drama — visual, aural. Split off, playing separately, overlapping.* Do Ko Do Ko Don Ka Ra. *Alternately leaping to the other side, backs to the audience. Is this where we converge?* Do Ko Do Ko Don Ka Ra. Do Ko Ko Don. *(If I weren't leaving town, if I'd been available to perform this — could I?)* Do Ko.

II

As of one mind, *kiai* / engaging abdominal
the diaphragm tightens, forced air
through the mouth / emit a muscled *yo*
feed our life force / a call for invention
adding impact / need a trick to *so-re*
at will / with as little throat
possible / our voices not only for words
sa sa sa / so simple we lose
our place / can't deny these cries
transformative / an argument
for practice / this isn't
second nature.

Ko

Another kind of vocabulary. Sharp, focused vocalizations typically sounded at random: an energy converged. How to cultivate the primal. I struggle to improvise meaningless sounds but never mind my self-consciousness; how do I stay on beat? Afraid of breaking sequence — but practice builds comfort, consistency, I suppose. Here's a way to activate intention, inhabit the present — the listener can hear it. Must I allow then that spirit generated by these guttural utterances drives dynamism, audience engagement? A means of keeping tempo, signaling to others. "Focus on quality of sound as it is produced and felt in the body." Interspersed with rhythms of drumming — a form of music linked to the evolution of social communication. All the while inherent in the undertaking: an emergent wildness.

Do

Consider the role of voice in Western literature and art, especially women's voice. Perceived as representative of "emotional excess and the irrational — a 'sound unmediated by language.'" Dangerous or transgressive, as a madwoman or siren. Forti's use of voice neither resists nor embraces these formulations but coexists with them. Where voice speaks "of the unspeakable, of signaling through the flames [...] untamed noise from the center of a burning pit, the living gut."

Ko

The dōjō *is a space where women are empowered, encouraged to exercise and communicate strength. Traditionally deemed incapable of meeting the physical demands of taiko, women's participation now likely exceeds that of men. And yet. Even recently some senior members of the Japanese taiko community adhere to the notion that performances by women featuring loud vocalization and forceful pounding of drums have "lurched [...] beyond the confines of properly gendered behavior [...] or, yet further, outside the genre of Japanese drumming itself." Are women who fully engage in all aspects of taiko, including boisterous vocalization, bound to be regarded merely as untamed, unfeminine, wild? And when such a performance style is considered acceptable, are women's voices permitted only because originally, such sounds were executed exclusively by men?*

Don

Forti's *Rollers* (1960): Two performers in wooden boxes with wheels and ropes attached; swiftly, wildly swung throughout a space. Improvising a duet of vocalizations. Voice employed in ways that trouble the boundaries between long-held "binary formulations in Western thought: the rational and the irrational, mind and body, culture and nature." Characterized by "a tension between the signifying work of language and the apparently lawless work of the body."

Ka

Forti's *Censor* (1961): A sound competition pitting a pan of nails, shaken, against a voice singing loudly, volume of both in balance. Eventually straining to a yell, unable to convey the song being sung. The voice, particularly the female voice, deployed in an unusual way. To Forti, the voice was the "perfect material with which to expose the body's powers and limits, as it was its more mobile, flexible counterpart."

Ra

Forti's *Accompaniment for La Monte's "2 Sounds"* (1961): A performer stands, spinning, in a loop of rope suspended from the ceiling, while a recording of Young's "2 Sounds" plays.[1] "The sound has an immediacy; it physically enters your body." Discordant, inducing sensory saturation, requiring a focused involvement in the moment. Forti notes, "an audience member can identify with me, and can experience my movement, and what I'm experiencing. I'm hoping that through my behavior as I perform, I'm opening that channel so that someone watching can experience it with me." Helping the viewer take in the situation, respond on impulse. In this dance of stillness, an invitation to hear something otherwise inaccessible. Observer as dancer as co-musician; listening as part of the making.

1 YVONNE RAINER: Performer in a loop of rope accompanied by La Monte Young's Two Sounds is one of my favorite Forti pieces —

II

of a body scored or sometimes
spontaneous / a melody sampled / we
circulate a phrase occurring in each
individual's extraction / riffed, in mirroring
cohere / count out allotted beats to echo
each our own iteration an energy interchange / we
solo in rotation, a current carried
through / tuned in, tagged to cue
entrance, return / in sync as any sequence
in unison.

Ko

What's a solo if not an invitation? Permission to step forward freely granted.
A fragment of a melody adapted; pass it around. Start simple, small,
something to fill eight beats perhaps, allowing such spin. To reinterpret
a rhythm yet maintain cohesion to a whole — as in a piece, as in the
ensemble. How to interweave phrases, make movements corresponding?
Vocally support each interlude, through the energy of kiai. *Each*
player attuned to the rest, each become part of a body in motion.

Don

Forti: "[Y]ou can be a group of artists who are paying attention to what everyone else is doing [...] that moment when an individual takes a solo and the others step back as a support. Then you sense when the solo is over, and you let that person join the support again."

Ko

Forti's *Cloths* (1967): From three square frames hang fabrics, stapled. Performers crouch behind, invisible to the audience. Intermittently flipping cloths to the fronts of their frames, until all are turned. Meanwhile. A recording of friends, as if hardly aware they are singing their favorite songs. Mixed with live singing, overlapping, echoing but also. Silences, periods when only one song is heard. Variations on a solo. Three gauging the appropriate moment to sing as well as when to flip their piece of cloth. A screen to "hide behind," concealment serving to disembody the voice from the performer. Running counter to long-held notions: woman's voice, particularly the singing voice, "regarded as embodied, redolent of the body from which it emanates."

Don

Rudimentary improvisation or an exercise in gauging connection, version two: Together in a circle, or aligned in rows. We drum. Start out very slow, very quiet, and over a period of minutes gradually pick up more speed, more volume, until we are all playing as loud, as fast as we can. We play for some time, then start to slow down. The slowing-down much faster than the speeding-up. Within this general speeding up, playing and slowing down, are several minor speed-ups and slow-downs. We finally come to a stop and take a water break.

Ko

What the body is capable of. Problems to solve, "explorations" to embark on. Prompted beyond plan or habit, expanding "movement vocabulary." The more explored, the more new, original material emerges. Every step off a curb, every fall of a leaf its own quality — to focus on this particularity to avoid discriminating against any gesture. A way of thinking with the body. When trying to understand how a situation will unfold, sensing how to verbalize the tension while also moving. To feel it in the body, express it also using the body.

Don

So much depends on observation, alertness to the subtle actions of fellow performers. But more than that. Immersion, through one's own body, in a way of being. Memory imbued in limbs.

And what of Sensei's proclamations about kinesthetic intelligence, seemingly inaccessible? My resistance borne of perceived inadequacy. I strive to let go of this notion, embrace possibility.

Out of the country, I miss the San Francisco World Percussion Arts Festival, Maikaze Daiko's performance of Requiem dei Tambori. *Yet then and now, I can't help but step through the movements in my mind, all the while wondering whether I could have executed the piece along with my collaborators, leaping through the aisles of drums, coordinating strikes, conjuring audience intrigue. I still have my doubts.*

I still envy others their physical explorations. That a tree's texture might "show up in the crinkling and flickering of the surface of one's back." *But I have my own ways of probing these intersections.* As a dancer's body is "precisely the site at which the radically other — such as a tree — might be apprehended, just as, in Young's music, it [is] through the body that the other worlds of sounds [are] best understood."

But I'm still listening. Receptive, wanting to open myself to what I hear. Which can lead to all sorts of surprising movements.

Notes

Each of the paragraphs in this essay represents a single drum strike from what was informally called the "center line" sequence of "Requiem." Each heading (*Don, Do, Ko, Ka, Ra*) indicates the type of strike — the sticking (which hand is used), volume, duration, and position on the drum (rim or head).

Do The idea of creating a scenario in which one could climb refers to Simone Forti's comments in Schlenzka (2016).

Ko Quote and adapted description of *Huddle* are from *Fondazione Furla* (2017), which discusses *Furla Series #01*, a reenactment of four performances marking fundamental points in Forti's career. Further description is adapted from Forti (1998, 59).

Do No specific references were used to create this passage.

Ko Quotes and adapted description are from Forti (1998, 29–31).

Do Quote by Simone Forti is from Forti (1998, 29–31).

Ko Material about the spinning techniques of dancers is from Murphy (2015).

|| No specific references were used to create this passage.

Do Description of and quotes about taiko warmups are from Powell (2006). Explanation of ki and the connection between player, drum, and audience is from the same source, based on the author's experience with San Jose Taiko.

Ko No specific references were used to create this passage.

Ko Material is adapted from Morse (2010, 122).

Don Description of Young's ideas on sound is from Morse (2016, 100). Explanation of the listener's role and response from critic John Perrault is adapted from Morse (2016, 66–67). Material on Forti's approach to sound is adapted from Morse (2010, 134).

Ko No specific references were used to create this passage.

Do Description of *See-Saw* is adapted from Morse (2016, 54).

|| No specific references were used to create this passage.

Ko Quotes and adapted material related to *Platforms* are from Morse (2016, 24, 97–100, and 121).

Do No specific references were used to create this passage.

|| No specific references were used to create this passage.

Ko Information about the history and evolution of drumming is from Wikipedia, s.v. "Drum," https://en.wikipedia.org/wiki/Drum. Definition of *kiai* is adapted from Enkamp (n.d.). Explanation of *kiai* is adapted from Rhythmyk (2009). Quote about the quality and feeling of *kiai* is from Powell (2006).

Do First quote and adapted explanation of perception of women's voice is from Morse (2016, 106–7). Second quote is by critic Jill Johnston, from Morse (2016, 57).

Ko According to Chan (2002), around two-thirds of North American taiko players today are women. Information about the explosion in women's taiko playing since the 1980s and 1990s is from "Women Unbound? Body and Gender in Japanese Taiko" (Bender 2012, chapter six). The quote in this section is also from Bender (2012, 164).

Don Adapted description of *Rollers* and quote about the female voice are from Morse (2016, 56). Quotes within the quote are by music scholar Freya Jarman-Ivens from *Queer Voices: Technologies, Vocalities, and the Musical Flaw.*

Ka Description of *Censor* is adapted from Morse (2010, 132). Quote explaining Forti's stance on voice is from Morse (2016, 97).

Ra Description of *Accompaniment for La Monte's "2 Sounds"* is adapted from Morse (2016, 96–97). First quote is by Tashi Wada, from Morse (2016, 94). Forti quote is from Forti (2018b).

|| No specific references were used to create this passage.

Ko No specific references were used to create this passage.

Don Forti's quote is from Schlenzka (2016).

Ko Description of *Cloths* is adapted from Forti (1998, 80). Ideas on the understanding of the female voice are from sound and media scholar Adriana Cavarero in *For More Than One Voice: Toward a Philosophy of Vocal Expression,* drawn from Morse (2016, 107).

Don No specific references were used to create this passage.

Ko Ideas about the body and movement are adapted from Forti (1998, 29) and from Forti (2018a).

Don The first quote by Forti and the second quote are from Morse (2016, 67).

UN/BOUND

We made this book out of a desire to learn more about and bring more attention to the work of Rainer and Forti. Beyond that, we felt a hunger for immersion in an absorbing project and a curiosity about how such immersion might impact us.

In our lives and art, we both privilege the role of relationship: relationship as conversation and debate; relationship as deep connection to art and ideas and the people who generate them; relationship as the interplay of words on a page; relationship to self as a construction, one to be held lightly and investigated continually; relationship to life itself in each changing moment.

The project we designed has allowed us to engage in our shared love of relationality along multiple vectors at once. We have savored and learned from the process of close collaboration, which ensures both a solid container for making work and (ir)regular doses of disorientation as one dances with another artist's particular mind. Our extensive research into Forti and Rainer's work has led us to experience both artists as active, mentoring presences in our lives. Through the elaborate process we constructed, which itself was grounded in our growing understanding of Forti and Rainer's ambitious and innovative approach to art-making, we have found ourselves interacting with the page and the world in surprising ways — entering zoos and dance studios to gather data, reaching out to old friends to check memories, and creating new formal containers for our words.

Changing the Subject: Learning from Postmodernism's Focus on Context

Sarah Rosenthal

Sometime in the mid-1990s, I had a phone conversation with my older brother David (who prefers the moniker DaveR), in which I shared my growing appreciation of New Music — avant-garde work influenced by John Cage, jazz, rock, Indian classical, and other musics from around the world. DaveR pushed back hard, going after the minimalist, conceptualist end of New Music represented most purely by Cage's piece *4′33″*, in which the composer sat silently at a piano for four minutes and thirty-three seconds — the music consisting of whatever ordinary sounds audiences heard as they squirmed their way through the piece (Hermes 2000). A classically trained pianist, DaveR resented what he considered a copout on the long hours of study and discipline required to be a "real" musician.

It's never been easy for me to take on DaveR. Even when I'm sure of my position, the intellectual guns he brings out are cannons. I regress to a state of angry kidhood, stabbing here, stumbling there, wearing myself down to, at best, a draw. In this case, I don't recall even trying to argue. I just didn't have the language to defend this music I was excited about.

And I felt a bit shaken. After all, we had grown up in the same family of classical music lovers. My maternal grandfather was a violist in the Philadelphia Orchestra and later tried his hand at composing. My paternal grandfather played the piano in an informal chamber ensemble that performed in various living rooms, most often that of a couple who lived in Chicago's Kenwood neighborhood — my parents had met at one of these gatherings. My father had the Chicago classical music station WFMT playing all day long — a vital form of self-medication for this driven, angry man. We all studied piano as children; DaveR really took to the instrument. One morning I awoke into the heart of a Johann Sebastian Bach piece he was practicing, flooded with bliss.

Yet, although my parents were passionate about classical music and the parallel versions of other art forms, they weren't stuck there. My father's business, making slides of art and architecture to be used by museums and universities, meant that he developed a familiarity with every visual-art epoch from the ancient to the contemporary. My mom, the bibliophile, read along a literary timeline spanning from the King James Bible through

Marcel Proust, James Joyce, and Franz Kafka. My parents didn't have, or at least didn't convey to us kids, a clearly articulated aesthetic. But I absorbed the message that art was worthwhile, period.

Prior to grad school, the arts education I gave myself was a wild quilt of influences and experiences. Yet while my quilt included canonized art and still does, I was slouching toward the avant-garde. Aurally speaking, I caught years of Charles Amirkhanian's music programming through the Berkeley-based KPFA station, along with a show by another KPFA host and musician, Carl Stone, who tweaked my ears weekly with fresh sounds. When I entered an MFA program in the mid-'90s, I dove into "experimental" literature, encountering brilliant innovators from Emily Dickinson, Walt Whitman, and Stéphane Mallarmé forward. I was just as excited by the work of my peers. And we were all ingesting innovations in other art forms.

You'd think by the time of the phone call with my brother, I'd have been able to make a case for New Music. But beyond the usual problem of sparring with someone better fit than I for the debate team, I saw DaveR's point. And the part of me steeped in the classical tradition agreed with him.

I changed the subject.

In the mid-'90s, I broke up with someone I'd been with for more than a decade. I'd been a nonconformist my entire life, and when my card-carrying radical partner had an affair and told me he'd assumed I was open to such things, I was ripped to shreds. Such an arrangement works well for some, but apparently I'm designed for dyads. The day after I found out about the affair, I bought lingerie and lipstick and decided that the next time around, I'd get married. I felt like I was bursting bonds. It wasn't rational — how can you call it a liberating move to embrace traditional behaviors and institutions you've spent a life resisting? And it's hardly as if marriage protects against infidelity. But in that moment, I saw that my former refusal to present myself as a sexual object had been built on a platform of fear — fear of men, of sex, of desire. This brittle platform had kept me from seeing myself and others clearly. DaveR agreed. Next time around, he advised, don't dismiss guys who aren't perfect on paper. Some of them may actually treat you better than X did, for all his stellar leftie credentials.

Lingerie and lipstick and marriage intrigued me precisely because they had seemed verboten. I was still a fierce feminist, but I was seeking a new subjectivity, one that involved more love, more risk, and fewer rules.

Sometime in the mid-'90s, I acquired a book on artist Marcel Duchamp. When I got to *Étant donnés*, a diorama witnessed through peepholes in a wooden door, I stopped cold. I was angered by the figure of a curvy, headless, spread-eagled nude who, except for the peculiar fact that her left hand holds a small lamp, easily evokes a (typically female) victim in a slasher movie. I also learned that Duchamp had used 1,000 foam-rubber breasts for the catalogue covers of the Paris exhibition *Le Surréalisme* in 1947. Even given his gender-bending adoption of alter ego Rrose Sélavy, he was tainted for me by these works that reinforced the history of women's subjugation. I shut the book.

❦

A decade after I decided that the next time I fell in love I would marry, I married. Once you sign up for that, you find yourself facing a whole series of symbolic objects and actions. For instance, I knew from the outset that I'd resist the white dress. I had in mind a certain cut — fitted empire waist, flowing long lines — and traipsed to one store after another, trying on myriad options in every color. None of them worked. I drew a sketch for a coworker; within seconds she had me on the J. Crew website looking at my dress. It was perfect — except it was white. The dress arrived in a thin box, fell onto me like a friend, hugged tight.

Off I went to the art store, picturing purple ribbons of many hues, widths, and textures streaming from the empire waist. A midsummer night's dream of a dress. But none of the artists who worked there bought in. None of my friends bought in. No one wanted to see me ruin a perfectly good wedding dress. Get a purple shawl, they advised. Get some big dangly earrings if you want. I did. Not much of a rebellion.

It all went like that. I had assiduously arranged things so I'd get a good night's sleep before the wedding, but by the wee hours I was in the midst of a major meltdown, having, as instructed by my doting future mother-in-law, just opened a gift box containing clip-on earrings and a matching necklace: enormous, round white pearls surrounded by little diamondy things. My partner said I absolutely did not have to wear them. But I spent the rest of the night trying to figure out how to explain to Muriel why I wasn't wearing her lavish gift, her invitation into a new level of intimacy.

I showed up at the wedding site late, with dark circles under my eyes. Hustling to the dressing room, I was greeted by exclamations of "*There* you are!" from those who had arrived early, as requested, to help. Eventually I found the friend who'd signed on to do my makeup, and who made no bones about her irritation at the fact that she now had to execute quickly. While she worked, I hastily slapped purple polish onto my nails, which only increased the tension, the toxic substance potentially endangering the health of the one-month-old fetuses which, in that moment, she revealed were growing inside her.

I had decided to have no one "give me away," but late in the game my dad had told me he planned to do so — my dad whose inappropriate sexual energy and verbal and physical abuse had been largely responsible for my adoption of a rigid definition of feminism. I recognized his eleventh-hour wish to inhabit the role of loving father and relented. We inched down the aisle to accommodate his increasing physical fragility, while DaveR played Minuet No. 1 of Bach's French Suite No.1 in D minor, BWV 812 — the same piece I awoke to hearing him play when I was a child in the '60s.

My partner waited for me under a chuppah because he was raised Jewish and because what's not to love about a chuppah — a little roof, open on the sides so everyone you love can surround and bless you. I circled him — the wrong number of times because I lost track. The ceremonial goblet we drank from was cracked; wine spilled blood-red down the center of my dress, so I got the avant look I'd wanted after all but was upset about it. But had to put on a happy face.

I'd suggested potluck; my beloved informed me that his people didn't do potluck. So we served homemade tuna salad and potato salad and three-bean salad on paper plates. But they were really weddingy paper plates.

A wedding's a wedding and it wears its history like a long white train. There's only so much I was going to disappoint a bunch of elders schlepping suitcases full of expectations across the country to attend our event. Still, we managed to mess with convention and implicate even our most mainstream guests in ways they hadn't expected, signing them up to help us make the aforementioned salads, move tables and chairs, and perform in or watch what amounted to a talent show, including a long rap in German by my German nephew, who apparently never got the memo that the performances were supposed to honor our betrothal. Every 50 words or so, he banged his fist against his chest and shouted *schiesse* at the top of his lungs. Shit. The guests sat bemused, probably wondering when their patience would finally earn them some coffee and cake.

Twenty-some years after I dismissed Duchamp because of artworks I found infuriating, I started studying the work of choreographer and filmmaker Yvonne Rainer. When I found out about Duchamp's impact on Rainer and her peers (mediated in part by Cage, who counted Duchamp and Zen Buddhism as his biggest influences, and who in turn significantly influenced Rainer's crowd), I took a fresh look at his aesthetic. I still don't know what to do with the slasher diorama or the 1,000 breasts, but I'm putting those pieces on the shelf for now. Viewing him through the work of later generations, I'm focusing on the fundamental shift he helped bring about in the way art is understood.

Through his "readymades," most infamously the urinal he titled "Fountain," Duchamp rejected what he called "retinal" art, or art designed for passive viewing. Instead, he wanted to instigate active thought in the viewer (Rosenthal 2004). I can now appreciate, thanks largely to Carrie Lambert-Beatty's book *Being Watched: Yvonne Rainer and the 1960s*, how he helped pave the way for works by Rainer and others that got viewers to think about their own perceptions and projections. Lambert-Beatty describes how these younger artists, inspired in part by Duchamp's stance, contributed to a shift,

> from a mindset that seeks art's essence in inherent aspects of the work, to one that finds art's definition contingent upon the structuring conditions of its appearance. How an object or event is seen — under what

> institutional conditions? Subject to what assumptions on the part of the viewers? And by viewers physically and socially positioned how? (2008, 38)

In other words, these artists' work challenged an idea that had long held sway. In this schema, the lone artist creates the masterpiece and presents it in a pristine setting where the humble audience comes to receive inspiration. By contrast, Rainer and her peers foregrounded the fact that art is never separate from the world; it is always made and shared in contexts that affect how we experience and interpret it. Such contexts include the setting or environment in which a piece is seen, the "institutional conditions" Lambert-Beatty speaks of — museum or mall, art gallery or corporate lobby, studio or street. They include the specifics of how viewers are permitted to engage with an artwork — must they stand behind a velvet rope, or may they clamber all over the piece? And the contexts include audience members' myriad assumptions and biases, based on such factors as race, class, gender, age, form of embodiment, education, location, and language.

Rainer's role in helping bring about this shift is easily evident in her work. Take *Hand Movie,* which she had a friend film in 1966 while she was stuck in a hospital bed convalescing after a surgery (Rainer 1966). Her right hand, upright in front of the white hospital wall and cut off below the wrist by the bottom of the screen, does a meditative dance. While in some respects the piece echoes Duchamp's diorama (a cut-off female body part), this unadorned hand is alive, agentic, and gender-neutral. The simple white frame in which the cut-off hand enacts its dance removes it from any familiar referents, creating a productive, Brechtian alienation that allows us to see it as a strange new object or body that can do its own kind of dance. We observe the small moves, projecting a potentially vast array of meanings onto the dancing hand over the course of the film: comedy, pathos, eroticism, friendliness, cool distance, mischief. In a mere eight minutes, we come to understand both the terms *hand* and *dance* in entirely fresh ways. The contrast between the minimalist, even stark, dance and the plethora of thoughts it triggers might lead us to reflect on our active role in determining the meaning of art. We might recognize that we and the beliefs and biases we bring with us are as important a part of the equation as that which we observe. And we might open ourselves to new ideas about what bodies and art can and can't do.

Or take the Vietnam War–era piece *Trio A with Flags.* Rainer came up with this version of her signature dance *Trio A* for the "People's Flag Show." Artists had been invited to show works incorporating the American flag, to protest the government's prosecution of a gallerist who had exhibited the work of a sculptor alleged to have desecrated the flag. Rainer and colleagues performed nude with large American flags tied around their necks (Lambert-Beatty 2008, 212). The flags both masked and revealed their nudity, potentially triggering an array of emotionally charged responses and the accompanying opportunity for self-reflection on the audience's part. The "institutional conditions" invoked include the flag as a symbol of democracy and freedom, the government's slaughter of innocent bodies and its simultaneous crackdown on freedom of expression in the name of this symbol, and the protest of these repressive acts. Beyond that, the piece confronted observers with widespread assumptions about the naked human body in art. If we accept as art's pinnacle the hundreds of years' worth of women's naked bodies painted by men, displayed in museums, and valued in the millions of dollars, what grounds could anyone conjure to name as inappropriate and repulsive the flashing of body parts from behind draped flags as the performers dance in the Judson Memorial Church auditorium in Greenwich Village? Does the exposure of the naked human body bear special relevance in the context of the Vietnam War, when so many came home in body bags? What are we free to express, under what circumstances, and to whom? How is this expression received and processed, by whom?

Such questions, which Duchamp helped foreground and which Rainer and her peers extended, are a gift that keeps on giving. Today, a couple decades into the new millennium, addressing the positioning and treatment of our bodies within various institutional conditions is as critical as ever. People of conscience continue to foreground fundamental questions about repression and freedom of these bodies, minds, hearts, and mouths of ours.

I got married on Saturday, May 26, 2006. I'd heard Madeleine Peyroux's exquisite, swinging rendition of Leonard Cohen's "Dance Me to the End of Love" and had a vision of my beloved and me improvising a flamboyantly expressive dance to it. The beloved felt that this would be disastrous, given our amateur dance skills. So we hired a dance teacher to help us choreograph the piece. It was a struggle for me to inhabit the follower role — this was why I hadn't wanted to marry a man in the first place — but we worked it out. On the wedding day we delivered perfectly, gesture after gesture to the dramatic last pose.

At this grand moment, when I'd envisioned all eyes trained unblinkingly on our performance, the energy of the reception had dissipated. A behind-the-scenes snafu in one of the performances had caused a stretch of dead time — enough that given all the other performances the guests had sat through by then, including the Shit Rap, they began to drift to the back of the auditorium to chat and drink coffee. Some folks simply up and left. By the time we walked onto the dance floor, only 20 or so people were watching us. (But they got more than they expected. In the few photos — and what's happened to the damn video?! — I see faces riveted, expressions almost disbelieving.)

For years after, I spent many a 3 a.m. soliloquy reliving the frustration that the experience had not gone as envisioned.

Since I began studying the choreography of Yvonne Rainer and her peers, the writing I've been doing in response has married this research in various ways to my own experiences of performance and dance. Given that my wedding was the most ambitious performance I've ever orchestrated, it feels right to revisit that event through the work and thought of these postmodernists.

Yet it's an awkward comparison at best. For all that Rainer and her colleagues helped broaden our understanding of what art can be, they were still working at a remove from the everyday world — they felt at liberty to develop and execute their artistic visions however they saw fit and as provocatively as they dared. I had to make — or felt I had to make — all kinds of compromises in the creation of the wedding in order to arrive at something everyone could find a way to relate to, from avant-garde poet friends to loving elders with their treasured beliefs and expectations.

But the ideas that Duchamp helped champion and that Rainer and her crowd extended in the context of '60s radicalism — and which continue to permeate art and thought — also give me a recuperative way to view our wedding, and in the process to tease out universals embedded in the event beyond something borrowed, something blue.

When I muse on the way Rainer and others helped create a shift "from a mindset that seeks art's essence in inherent aspects of the work, to one that finds art's definition contingent upon the structuring conditions of its appearance" (Lambert-Beatty 2008, 38), I realize how limited my post-wedding analyses have been. I've congratulated us over and over on the parts that went well and wrung my hands about what went poorly. But with the help of these avant-garde artists, I can focus on the structural conditions surrounding this event, and as a result am no longer inclined to assign grades. Rather, I now focus on the ways the event was embedded in a set of conditions and assumptions determined by a vast array of institutional, cultural, political, and economic constraints. It could not have been any other way than exactly as it was, a flawed work of art in which every guest was a participant.

DaveR and Bach collaborate to open the floodgates to feeling. Soggy Kleenex absorbs tears of red-nosed listeners as my partner and I read aloud our vows — vows my father will later tell me he read at home afterward, weeping his heart out, that heart so long buried under a narcissistic rage that had constantly threatened to destroy everyone in our family and to some extent succeeded, that heart that never stopped secretly pulsing with paternal love. Scarlet wine spills down my white dress, comically making the point that I'm no pristine virgin, while evoking the passion and pain that are part of any long-term romantic commitment. My nephew shouts "Shit! Shit! Shit!" — unrelentingly forcing us to acknowledge yet another bodily excrement that reminds us of the animals we are even when dressed to the nines, and making the event a performance Karen Finley might admire. Well-off conventional elders and poor avant-garde poets alike wander to the back of the room to stretch stiff limbs and find cake at exactly the moment their bodies need it, leaving a devoted few to be inspired and maybe forever just slightly altered by our perfectly executed dance to the end of love.[1]

1 YVONNE RAINER: Interesting: The wedding as a flawed work of art beyond your control —

OFF THE PEDESTAL

In the spirit of collaboration, we decided to reach out to Rainer and Forti, to engage them directly in this project. Forti attended a reading we gave in Los Angeles and encouraged the endeavor. It was magical to spend an evening with someone whose oeuvre we'd been studying intensively, and to experience first-hand the acute attention to the world and low-key yet sparkling presence that we had sensed in her work. She also shared written feedback on one of the essays in the book, which prompted a significant revision of that piece.

Rainer read the full manuscript and sent a spirited list of comments in response to specific phrases and passages. True to her radical aesthetic, she suggested that we respond to her comments and publish the whole:

> *I think it might interest a reader to have your addenda following a particular YR note: eg: if you remove references to the NO Manifesto as I suggested (It's up to you), you might indicate that either in an introductory note or a parenthetical explanation beside my own note! I hope that is not too complicated — I have confidence that you will figure it out — I look forward to the publication — Yvonne*

We were intrigued by this collaborative approach — and eager to address a few issues in our essays that she felt misrepresented her work. We recognized that an artist with a career as long as Rainer's can come to feel trapped by early works and statements that become calcified as they are passed from one art critic to the next. We revisited and analyzed every instance in the collection related to the concerns she expressed, which led to many revisions. Once we had done that, we addressed Rainer's comments in footnotes that appear throughout the collection. Rainer's reference to addenda refers to a format we considered and ultimately discarded.

This interchange underscored for us Rainer's commitment to innovation, while her responses conveyed the intelligence, conviction, curiosity, and humor that permeate her work and personality. It's not what we expected — and exactly what was needed.

Brutality of Borders: Experiments with Narrative or How One Thing Follows Another

Valerie Witte

"There's always a lot of brutality." One foot crossed over the other, a kick forward, kick back, four alternating steps. *Retreat, attack, retreat, attack.* Why is dance so difficult to explain? If we had more words for hop, or step, or one-two-three-four. The five steps always begin the same way. *When executing a gesture too intimate to my body, I fragment it or throw it away.* Begin with the right, repeat on the left. The last part always the same. There's always a lot of repetition. The repetition of always always sounds suspicious. *Reality is patternless despite our attempts to graft stories onto experience.* Yet the instinct to make sense, something orderly, nothing left to chance. I try building in chance. *Do away with predictability of structure, demands of a frame.* Transcribe a *News Animation,* using only what I can type in the time I hear it spoken, enacted. A process inherently, inevitably, flawed. I slice text into fragments, weave them through. I was eight, maybe nine — a birthday, eight becoming nine. Assuming this was third grade, as I recall. I want to get the details right. Don't want to mislead anyone, i.e., you, the reader. I was part of a quartet of girls performing an Irish jig for the annual school talent show. Is this the only time I've voluntarily participated in a choreographed dance? Whole-heartedly, enthusiastically. *Let's try to fill in the gaps.* I remember practicing a lot — for months before the show, which took place in spring. I wore black Isotoner slippers; a green, decorative skirt; and, I think, a white blouse. I'm trying to foreground objects, a challenge this many years out. *But the roots, they go down deep.* "Strawberries send out runners," as if strawberries were sentient, aware that messing with the neighbor's yard is potentially problematic. Isn't it nice that the word "neighbor" has such a positive connotation, though its origins simply mean "dwelling near"? Do the strawberries have a sense of where they are heading? My mother would have photos in the basement to resolve all this. I was on stage right, though I doubt I knew the term. *I want to be seen in several, not always corresponding, dimensions.* This is my only positive memory of performative dance. Though this experience thereby disrupts my narrative, I choose to include it. *There is no seeing that is not the result of a mode of reading that both reveals and conceals.* "In Australia you'll see more stars because you're looking at the center of our galaxy. The edge of the arm and the whirling. It would be this way. Or would it?"

As I was saying, auditions were required, and we made the cut. Not sure when, I'm guessing fall? If I write "Shortly after the fall of Soviet Europe, there were pockets of different languages" here, I must ignore that it doesn't fit the chronology of my story. (By my math, three more years till that collapse.) In producing this collection, in building and playing out the process in which we deliver prompts to each other, and respond: simultaneous embrace and dismissal of narrative. Understand what I am recounting is based on recollections from more than thirty years ago. *Retrieving images from the borders of memory. But roots run deep.* The other girls — Michelle, Bridget, Sweetie — were Irish, had taken dance classes for years. I invited them over for a birthday sleepover — February then — ostensibly to practice. But also: I wanted to be friends with two of them. It is hard to resist the comfort of categories. "I'm with my friend Nora; is my friend Nora still here?" Who decides? *We are entering a strange in-between state.* When what's nebulous is preferable, or merely what's available. All this time, I've understood *Irish jig* as the name of the specific dance we performed but now realize, of course, it's simply a catch-all term for the style. Stepdance is characterized by a rigid upper body, intricate footwork. High on the balls of the feet. Who makes these determinations? "People make borders where they want borders." Once defined, what separates an idea, a perspective, a place, or a form from another is still arbitrary. Because venues were small, they danced on tables or the tops of barrels. There are many ways to imitate a flattened experience. *Where nothing matters, equally.* Yet that "feeling when you're the biggest, that is who you are." Stories we tell ourselves, about ourselves, or that are told to, about, or around us, by those who mock or bully us. Who love us. "Nora left yesterday," we come to find out. This, too, has roots. A classic Irish name or: derived from the Latin, "honor." Who's to say? But some truths are unequivocal. "In a castle. A beautiful crown of a saint, a political figure at the same time. Would this also be the crown of my saint and my king?" I don't mean for this piece to be political. But Simone Forti's *News Animations* are. Translating the language of news stories into improvised movements. She might say that's exactly the point. I don't really think she would say that. Now what? "Ever notice that Trump looks a lot like Mussolini?" *Things that go up might one day fall.*

How I'm shy: a story I've internalized, clung to, though I don't like what it suggests, nor the way this perception has held me, held me back. And another, one I've told myself: that I can't dance. This experience of the jig doesn't fit the narrative I've constructed. I try re-entering the brain of eight-to-nine-year-old-me. *Autobiography proves an anti-sentimental twist. A plot imbued with tension, suspense mixed with the direct, factual quality of intimacy.* Of knowing. Must a body be readable? "She says no. We don't know the histories of the people we impact." I am half-Sicilian, half-German. This, too, is a story. But accepting this premise further complicates my motivation. What led me to perform such a routine with three Irish dancers?

Why did I think I could? Maybe a dance is just a dance. Not a journey or a revelation. No climactic event, no turning point in which the trajectory of my life shifted dramatically. I did not change. I am not aware of any changing. *As if reading from a diary, while others produce an effect of nothing happening.* I performed the jig and to my recollection, I did it well. I feel the impulse to qualify this assessment, as usual; what I think I remember is that I did not do badly. Nothing indicates I did it badly. So now what? This jig, of course, was nothing if not traditional. Codified, systematized. Why does standardization sound so sad? Don't worry, I come to these findings by googling. Derived from French quadrilles, English country dancing in the eighteenth, nineteenth centuries. Preserved, promoted, part of a nationalist movement. Yay, let's erect more walls around ourselves. "And these histories entwine, any movement seen so differently. Any movement is part of that history is part of that story is part of what matters or doesn't matter. Honor before life, or a kind of behavior toward the scriptures, the scriptures, the scriptures." Talk about questionable stories. A few years ago, in a training session my partner arranged for me and three friends. *Emotional or narrative content kept elusive, fragmented. Meaning played out in several, not always corresponding, dimensions.* Am I trying to subvert the story? "Have you ever had an herb garden? The wars, the territorial wars in the herb garden." I don't mean to subvert the story. We keep looking for ways to build, secure borders. Then tear them down and start over — as long as someone else is paying. The roots run deep.

So now what? That my partner arranged this for the people he loves is telling. He wanted me to learn a kind of language, access a common vocabulary. *These constructions hover somewhere within the borders.* "Within which everybody believes the same, lives the same, with a lot of brutality." Or conversely, a shorthand to navigate conflict. *Until stuttering creates its own dynamic.* Communicating through gesture, maybe a light jig. *Accompanied by rekindling of interest in narrative structures.* Place weight on your left foot, hop once, kick the right foot forward, then back, shift weight onto right — step left, right, left. *Things that go up must eventually come down.* Hop, hop back. Hop on your right foot. Shift weight, left-right-left-right. *Why are these instructions so difficult to understand?* How we tell our stories. *Experiences rushing in to fill the vacuum.* "As oregano sends runners into its neighbor's earth — sprout up in the middle." When we're called upon to question what we've come to believe about ourselves. I still have the journal where I recorded my notes; I wonder where it is. The trainer told me I'm a tiger. Which reminds me of the old Frosted Flakes jingle. *Where did that come from? I'll use that.* Or was it lion? *Belly like a bellows.* "Just get bigger, just get bigger." Which calls to mind *Sleepwalkers/Zoo Mantras,* Forti's studies of animal movements in Rome. *In circling, the elemental repetition and giving in to momentum to induce an altered consciousness.* "But if you're looking in, you really see the Milky Way, you really see it." "As strawberries send out runners to where there's space and those send out runners. Go, go." Like a tiger. *Is this a narrative reborn? A deliberate dismantling of defined structures.* What she said I interpreted to mean I am strong, can be bold, have potential for greatness. "Once I saw a little place in the dirt move, put in my hand and pulled up a big toad. Go, go." What could go wrong? "So ISIS wants a Caliphate." *Nothing matters, not too much anyway. Because everything matters, equally.* Or maybe she meant I'm solitary yet social. A good swimmer. Or can roar. Yes, this. I love that she said this, all it suggests. But this understanding, this notion of self is a different story, one I've never internalized. What happens if I keep digging? I could surely clear this up by checking that journal. *These roots run deep.* Now I remember counting: The jig has five steps. Hop, hop back, hop back two-three-four. Then repeat it all on the opposite side.

On the grid I've made on my back patio, I execute (attempt) the steps of the jig. I remember some but not all the steps. One, two, three, five. Or is it one, two, four, five? *Should I be ensuring that you, reader, can put together enough elements to get some kind of message? Or present a variety of experiences which you are free to interpret, select from, absorb?* "When Mussolini said, 'Yes, I ordered that assassination and I'm ready to do more of the same.'" *One thing follows another.* Is there a concluding section to the dance, which brings together everything we've performed up to this point? I remember church hymns, TV jingles from the '80s, parts of old hand-clap games, sign language for the chorus of a Christian pop song. I don't remember this much of any other combination of movements. I'm impressed I remember most of the steps. *The roots run deep.* Disappointed I remember most but not all the steps. What strikes me when re-creating what I can of the jig now is how immediately exhausted I become. Once through and I'm breathless. Which inevitably becomes part of my narrative. I don't recall feeling this way when I was eight. Now what have I revealed? In a certain context, under the right circumstances, at a specific point in time, it is possible to learn a particular kind of choreography. Wonder why I've never been able to replicate this seemingly happy sequence of steps. I mean events. I'm not sure if this is a question or whether I have an answer. *How one thing follows another.* "In Italy, every city has its tower and every family is fighting each other." If I'm being honest, I'm not sure I want to include "The young girls die in childbirth." But I'm trying to stay true to this story, which isn't entirely mine. This is where it ends. This is where the story is supposed to end, but this is a bleaker conclusion than I've prepared you for or that my story warrants. How about this: That dancer I met at a bar last year in Portland (which sounds romantic but isn't) said anyone can dance — you just need motivation. In third grade maybe I was motivated by the prospect of friendship. Remember: *One thing follows another. Whenever I'm in doubt I think of that.* But sometimes a dance goes nowhere. Sometimes a person becomes a frenemy or a nemesis. Sometimes we "make borders where we want borders." No matter how they shape our narrative. So now what? "In samurai movies, when they fly through the air and clash their swords and twirl away. Underwater, the beautiful trails following."

Notes

Italicized material is adapted from Banes (1987); Bennahum, Perron, and Robertson (2017); Morse (2016); Forti (2015); and Kotz (2014). The language is from the authors themselves, or quotes by the following: composer Tashi Wada, art critics Jill Johnston and Peggy Phelan, writer and critic Claudia La Rocco, Simone Forti, and Yvonne Rainer.

Content that appears in quotes is adapted from Fondation PHI (2016). Forti developed the concept for her *News Animations* in the mid-1980s. They involve a largely improvisational translation of news articles related to current events. In these works, as Forti explains, "Moving and speaking became a method of inquiry and social commentary, implementing all words that come to mind. These words arise from questions, feelings and speculations about the world brought to us by the news" (Fondation PHI 2016).

According to Morse (2016), "And now what" is a quote by Simone Forti from her *News Animation* at Bennington College in 2003.

"One thing follows another" is a quote from Rainer describing Forti's approach in which there is no attempt to connect events in a piece thematically (Lambert-Beatty 2008, 140–41).

DEAR READ DARE

Juxtaposing our own memories related to dance with Rainer and Forti's choreography has given us a greater appreciation for the conditions that have shaped our relationships to dance and to our bodies, and a greater sense of freedom in the ways we move through the world. We hope that your engagement with these essays serves as a stimulus to further develop your own relationships: to the work of these supremely important artists, to other artists and art forms that excite you, and to the exquisite and ordinary dance you do every moment of every day.

How Will You Move: Including All of Us in the Dance

Saran Rosenthal

To the reader,

In the spirit of the postmodern choreographers whose work helps inform this essay collection, *How Will You Move* balances constraints with chance procedures. There's a section for each letter of the alphabet (constraint), but I randomized the order of the letters (chance). I wrote the sections in the same sequence in which they appear here, my vision and understanding growing in dynamic relation to the piece's evolution.

Another constraint: each letter-section includes a reference (initially explicit; later on sometimes quite oblique or gestural) to each of the following: Yvonne Rainer's dance piece *The Concept of Dust*, John Prendergast's book *In Touch*, and the dance class I've been taking at ODC Dance Commons in San Francisco, as well as instructions (or in dance parlance, a score) for dancing that letter (again, sometimes explicit, sometimes oblique). Houselessness entered in of its own accord (chance, again).

Ever since I started this piece, I've been referring to it as an *abecedarium*. I was thinking that was the word for the poetic form in which each line, stanza, or section in some way responds to or focuses on a letter of the alphabet. Harryette Mullen's *Sleeping with the Dictionary* is a contemporary exemplar of this form, which dates back to ancient texts including King David's Psalm 118 and Chaucer's "An ABC." It turns out the correct word is *abecedarian*. Someone tried to tell me this, I now realize, but I blocked my ears, in love with the hum of "um." An *abecedarium*, according to Merriam-Webster, is an alphabet primer.

Is *How Will You Move* a poem or a primer?

r

Or a choreography. To make **r**, start upstage right. Proceed straight toward the audience. Assume proscenium. Blinded but focused. Reverse before you stumble on stage lights. Retrace. Almost complete the path back; bank toward upstage left. Grace a shallow curve.

r is for dancer-choreographer Yvonne Rainer. Father, Joseph, born Guiseppe Rainero, balanced half-naked on a buddy's shoulders on a California beach, 1922. Emigrated from the old country, met and married fellow Italian Jew Jeannette Schwartz in San Francisco. Jeannette felt overwhelmed by parenthood. She and Joseph farmed out four-year-old Yvonne and her brother to a foster care establishment for children of single moms. Three years of corporal punishment, Sunday afternoon visits. But Jeannette was the one who enrolled her daughter in ballet classes, took her to the opera, and later, when Yvonne was a struggling New York artist, sent cash. Jeannette and Joseph were both passionate anarchists. "From the age of twelve I had [...] been exposed to the heady comingling of poets, painters, writers, and Italian anarchists who gathered at the Workman's Circle in the Fillmore district every Friday night to hear the likes of Kenneth Rexroth, Kenneth Patchen, Herbert Read, and George Woodcock read poetry and socially critical essays."[1]

Listen to the letter the whole way through. Let it resonate, the sound massaging your body as you move across the floor. This is your score. **r** is your partner. If you start moving and **r** doesn't choose to accompany, abandon the gesture.

Learn the latter approach from Rainer, whose dance *The Concept of Dust* enacts an attentive anarchism, freedom to try but fail to enlist the aid of another, to flail and fall in slow motion while a found partner pillows you.

Abandon the gesture but not the letter.

Nor the woman at the corner. Pass her most days when leaving the dance studio. She paces and freezes in every weather. Red fitted jacket, swollen red feet encased in found flats. "We try to hold ourselves up and in."

How to pillow her?

---

1 YVONNE RAINER: My father balancing in swimsuit on a buddy's shoulders was in California, not Italy — He met my mother, Jeannette, in San Francisco; she had migrated from New York, where she was born — He early on changed his name to Joseph Rainer from Guiseppe Rainero, thinking he was "Americanizing" it!
AUTHOR: The passage has been revised to reflect Rainer's comment.

o

Cookie said find your joy and dance that. She made a gathering motion to show how she gathers, gathers it into herself, energetic joy.

She feeds herself with her own name, the double **o** in Cookie.

Shot out a fearless leg; said, picture kicking Kavanaugh in the groin. And this other kick defends against your midnight street attacker. I could do it, side of the head. Look at my bruise, it's been a hard week, I'm a witch, come watch me.

This bruise spreading halfway down my calf. The yellows and greens, the purples.

The **o** in incommensurate. "When I first dropped into it, it was relational."

If anyone will protect the woman on the corner, it's Cookie or the Cookie in me. Where does the woman on the corner find food? Where does she sleep? How does she stay out of incessant rain?

Note to self: **o** self: Inquire with X the expert on services.

Incommensurates. Up to you to connect them how you will. In *The Concept of Dust,* Yvonne Rainer paces among the dancers with a handheld mic. At odd moments she or a dancer reads from a selected hodgepodge: ancient Mideast history, the diary of a Nazi doctor, a dream of an encounter with composer John Cage. "The readings appear in this disconnected way and I like that randomness."

A circle on the stage. You decide the size. To start, position yourself anywhere on the imaginary **o** and travel its circumference.

o is the **o** in the how of how will you move as you make this circuit.

"Anyone in the group can answer this."

b

How is and is not my or your or Yvonne Rainer's body like the body of the woman who lives outside the dance studio? She freezes in place, pressing nostrils with both hands. Trying to keep something in? Out? Kitty-cornered parents chat, check cells, waiting for kids to emerge from ballet. She resembles them today in a red, fitted down jacket, black jeans. A tattoo like a frieze adorns her ankle.

"Rainer's choreography of primary gestures and interrelations transposed elements of New York City's complex network of pedestrian activity into the theater frame and so dramatised the question of individual agency and society."

Mission District intersection. Extremes of up and down in somatic relation. Young parents' eyes and ears adroitly averted, every move shaped by a houseless woman's hollow gaze, bloated face. All participants costumed in fitted down jackets, flats, skinny jeans, tattoos. I implicate, implicate myself, strolling through, my clutch of random sources, my fantasy handheld.

"Take a few deep breaths and let your attention settle down and into your body."

Or into hers. What could she use? Inflatable pillow? Red rain poncho? Protein bars? Think of things flat and small, easy to carry.

Score in the key of **b** minor: Picture the stage as a street corner. Begin at the curb closest to the studio; cross directly toward the woman. Hesitate. Reverse. Circle the intersection, a curving jaywalk. Watch, look, and listen so as not to break. End up back at the woman.

Introduce yourself. Say, what is your name?

e

To fill a stage with **e**, start stage right and move in a straight line stage left. Abruptly turn upstage left. Start a circle banking through upstage center and continuing. Before you complete the circle, stop short.

"Beckett said all art is the same: to fill an empty space."

e for ellipse or elapse. A week has passed since I met Amy. She tugged a length of translucent plastic, a bag or a piece of tarp, between her hands, paced the sidewalk outside the park fence. Scurried past, flashing a smile of friendship? Of fear? Muttered her name: Amy. Muttered her home: I stay with a friend. The black spots on her teeth I mistook a quick second for braces. My privileged frame. Departed from her side, into the studio.

e ran to meet me in the dance. I didn't know their exuberance, their eagerness to engage. Cookie made of us a circle surrounding three dyads who improvise contact in the center. Anyone could cut in at any time, no etiquette. **e** rushed to interrupt, marvelous error, fleeting partner. For days I felt the whirlwind.

"The invisible, although it keeps itself hidden, makes itself felt." Silent **e**.

j

I pulled **j** from a glass dish, unfolded and read it.

j brings heartbreak. But it's not **j**'s fault. "Random structure of the dance." **j** showed up; I never asked for **j**. I mean, I wasn't born knowing about **j**.

A person wrote **j** on a slip of paper, folded it, placed **j** and its twenty-five closest relations in a dish's hollow curve. That former me created a score. Current me randomly selected **j** and now meaning is made.

And meaning just now is "dark and pessimistic." I didn't ask for everything that is. The everyday movements of people in dynamic opposition at a street corner in a so-called "changing neighborhood." Class polarization affecting every gesture.

j manifested in my world. "Wounds to the heart are usually relational in origin." That describes my connection to **j**, all right.

I'm not going to tell you where to start. Jump from the dot your body makes across empty space to begin your line. Continue for a time in a direction. Swerve toward your own right. Skid to a halt.

I didn't ask for **j** any more than I asked Rainer and her cohort to investigate ordinary movement, which, if you take it seriously, makes you look at bodies on a street corner. I might not even have taken on Rainer if I'd known more about her. Because once I started to read up, I struggled to find a resonance. I had judgments — "She's conceptual and I'm not"; "I'm into embodiment and she's not." Eventually, this union arranged by chance revealed that we're both both and so much more. But for a time, I pummeled myself for having committed to a subject of study simply because I liked the sound of her name, Yvonne Rainer. I liked the sound of Judson Dance Theater with its prominent **j**. I wouldn't have started dancing at the studio in the "changing neighborhood" if it weren't for my investigation of Rainer and her colleagues. It felt like a logical extension. I wouldn't have seen a particular woman in diagonal tension from young parents checking cells, waiting for their kids to emerge from ballet. I wouldn't have introduced myself. It felt like a logical extension. And now I know we will never have a full-fledged conversation. She will never be able to grant me the right to include her here. She will never read this. Suspiration escapes. Escapes me.

f

In what Yvonne Rainer and others call the "final tableaux" of the 2015 MoMA performance of *The Concept of Dust*, the dancers take a series of prolonged poses, leaning on and pulling against one another while focusing their gaze on the audience, seated proscenium-style along one side of a square platform originally intended to display sculptures. The music that accompanies most of the piece has ended. Between that and the dancers' stillness, we enter a state of profound silence, one in which the sculptures breathe and return our stare. Call it a feminist vision of what sculpture can be.

Or call it an exploration of the final stage of life. The subtitle of the piece is *How Do You Look When There's Nothing Left to Move?* Rainer started work on this piece in her 80s; as of this writing, she's approaching 90.

Call it a capacity to stay in time's flow. Rainer's early *Trio A* assiduously avoids eye contact with the audience, resisting the impulse to pander or seduce. In this and many other ways, Rainer broke with the tenets of classical and modern dance, cracking open questions artists still inhabit, just as *Trio A* continues to be performed and taught.[2] But she's not stuck. In *The Concept of Dust* (which continued to morph for a time after the MoMA performance, with a new subtitle: *Continuous Project — Altered Annually*), she explores the capacity of the gaze to provide a profoundly moving experience of interconnection.

"We may call it friendship, but it is really a dynamic mystery, a lively, unfolding, open-ended process of listening, sharing, and discovery."

f is for final, feminist, flow. And f is for found, as in, having found Rainer through instinct and happenstance, I've devoted countless hours to studying her work and words. Found, as in, Rainer's practice of accompanying movement with the reading aloud of found texts. As in, her use of everyday gestures. Think street corner. Think houseless woman stock-still or pacing. Kitty-cornered parents loitering outside kiddie ballet. Me passing through en route to studio. Removing shoes, finding a spot, stretching alongside others, each of us preparing for the dance.

Start just barely upstage left of center; arc upstage toward stage left; then travel toward the downstage edge. Find your way back near the beginning of the straight part and trace a short line intersecting perpendicular. What found gestures might you fold in?

---

2 YVONNE RAINER: Please erase all mention of the No Manifesto! It lost its relevance 55 years ago, for me at least —
AUTHORS: In the version of the collection Rainer read, two essays quoted her 1965 manifesto in its entirety. Neither instance was critical to the meaning of the essays and both have been removed. In addition, prompted by Rainer's request, we examined her 2008 revision, titled "A Manifesto Reconsidered," and made sure that we are representing her more recent thinking as reflected in the latter. We encourage readers to look up Rainer's 2008 revision and examine how her thinking has evolved over time.

x

"Nobody wants crossed-out girls around," writes Fanny Howe, in a book partly about May, a houseless woman.

May and Amy share more than a corner of an alphabet.

When I read Howe's line "Only labor cares about her body in the world," I think, the system deems houseless people useless because by and large they're not producing; therefore, the powers have no incentive to solve the problem.

Mushrooming population. I find myself normalizing. "Well, at least they're under this bridge." (This very noisy bridge with exhaust coughing off it.) "Well, at least they're out of the rain." (If the tent doesn't leak and the air doesn't freeze.) "Well, at least they're together in their own little city." (Why not ask if I can move in?)

Howe inhabits May but I don't dare speak for Amy. Howe the radical political Christian strikes me as close enough pals with the people's Jesus for such a gesture. And Amy has spoken only six words to me. "Amy. I stay with a friend."

I had to stop going to dance class six weeks ago due to my job.

To make this letter, cross a person out. You know how. If not, I can guide you. It's called forgetting.

Or exploiting, like a good capitalist. "I ran the risk of being a puppet master or something." If I use a houseless person to make art, an object I sign with my own name, that's the opposite of advocate.

"The more we take ourselves and others to be objects, the further away from home we are." That means all of us. But while I am always in danger of losing my spiritual home, I still have a physical one.

y

Why use scores for dances? Isn't a "score" the notation for a piece of music?

Yes. The notion of scoring dances is something Yvonne Rainer learned from composer John Cage and his protégé Robert Dunn as well as from movement artist Anna Halprin. A handy term for a set of rules for making dances anyone can implement. A surefire way to break from tradition, as in Cage's famous score for his composition *4′33″*, which comprises four minutes and thirty-three seconds of the sounds the audience hears while the pianist sits still at the piano. Some in the audience heard for the first time: mutter of irate neighbors, snore of bored ones, electric hum of air conditioner, whimper of a pup tied up outside.

John's partner in life and art, choreographer Merce Cunningham, looked askance, not at John but at Yvonne and her peers. "As Cunningham always said, we were John's children and not his. And he made some disparaging remarks about what we were doing," she said. Maybe that disapproving glance gave impetus: "I studied with Merce for eight years and took ballet classes. But very early, I knew that I would not be accepted in any professional dance company, and that if I wanted to continue dancing, I'd have to make my own work."

"Score" has become common dance parlance. In class, teacher Cookie said, "A score is a form, an invitation, a limitation that invites sensation." For example, in *The Concept of Dust* the dancers follow a complex score with various choice points. One rule allows a dancer to press a pillow into another dancer. This triggers release of the recipient's weight into the pillow and awkwardly down to the floor, where the dancer rests momentarily before both segue.

y score for dance: Start upstage right. Head for the center and cross it. Now you have a choice. Will you turn 45 degrees and travel the same distance to upstage left, then reverse, pass the bottom of the v-shape you've made, end up downstage right? Or will you move to that latter point first, then reverse and head to the stage-left tippy top of your y?

Another day Cookie said, "Find your joy. That is one of the hardest scores to give."

Give me a score for the "beehive / here inside my heart." Make "white combs / and sweet honey / from my old failures."

l

Easily mistaken for uppercase I, lowercase l tells a different story. Two together form a parallel, like Cunningham and Cage, slender artists with good posture, paired for half a century.

"So I find I can still — I can't do much but then you start — and this comes directly from Cunningham — the feet are doing one thing and the body is doing something else, not related, and so we start patching stuff together."

Vertically and serially, Rainer is drawn to parallels. Like Cunningham and Cage, Rainer's peer Simone Forti "made no effort to connect the events thematically in any way [...] one thing followed another. Whenever I am in doubt I think of that. One thing follows another."

This uppercase I treasures the lowercase l in *vulnerable*, a word one might use to describe Rainer revealing her process. Not the chest-pounding auteur but someone who finds her way out of doubt, finds a serviceable way forward. Someone who patches together ideas, source materials, and body movements as part of a *we*.

Not that anything goes. She has called herself a "pretty tyrannical dictator." Noise from a video playing elsewhere in MoMA during the 2015 performance of *The Concept of Dust* elicited her irritation. Later, during the Q&A, she was asked to compare herself to Cage, who welcomed every sound as part of the performance. She said simply: "I'm not as democratic as Cage was." When critic Douglas Crimp wondered whether the dancers had contributed material to the piece, her immediate response was a blunt "No." Then she morphed: "They keep bringing in stuff."

When someone has examined uppercase I as much as Rainer has — let's just say she's put in her time on the analyst's couch — you don't ding her for holding onto the tiller. Consider the lowercase l in *valid*. Rainer embraces collaboration more than many. Does that mean she must relinquish individual vision? She has something particular to see, to say. When she surrendered to pure improvisation in the ensemble Grand Union, she couldn't participate without getting stoned. After two years of that, and for many reasons besides loss of artistic control, she segued to filmmaking for the next quarter-century. Since 2002, she's back to making dances.

How to hold all this data plus everything else uppercase I feels bound by? "Consider how you subtly tighten up when you are about to cross a busy street and how you relax once you have crossed."

z

"We started with a warm-up
facing the mirror. Cookie had us do
jazz-dance-type isolations
— blissed-out reaction."
"Clearly, there is some center
of feeling that localizes in
the center of the chest."
"We rolled our spines down,
hung, swayed side to side,
then rolled back up? I'm
hazy on the sequence.
Started moving in space,
just a little, then moreso."
"What has happened
here, and I realized how
important it is to this event,
[are] the relationships that
emerge among the dancers,
between them and me, so
we are a social entity and
that is very much part
of the whole evening."
"Groups of five across the
floor. Cookie asked us to
make eye contact while
dancing, relate energetically.
I was mostly focused on
learning the score — but some
motions did get internalized."
"Across 15th Street an
elaborate home: bed under
tarp strung as canopy; other
spaces along chain-link
fence have different functions,
like rooms. Proprietor
organizing his stuff. I think
of saying hi but refrain — he's
busy and I wasn't invited."

k

'Tis double death to drown in ken of shore. The rains keep coming. "Gotta be global warming," thinks Not-OK Katie, says it out loud, unwilling to let anyone feel less haunted than she does. Tents with tarps secured over them spring up like mushrooms. Citizens help citizens find shelter. If you're a petite 30-something woman living on the street, lacking kin factually or functionally, you're lucky if a tented friend gives you a corner to kip down in the dark. Days you kick around, days kick you around, as you seek a smoke or some small moment.

Walking to dance class under drizzle, I spot Amy puffing away intently, facing the café kitty-cornered.

Reagan called ketchup and relish vegetables. *He ten times pines that pines beholding food.* Through a café picture window "in the heart of the San Francisco Mission," denizens of the street behold a popular brunch option: thick-cut batard layered with butter, avocado, and a soft-boiled egg.

Kickshaw, from *quelque chose,* a little something. A fancy dish cum comfort food. *To see the salve doth make the wound ache more.*

"September 6, 1942. Today, an excellent Sunday dinner. Tomato soup, one half chicken with potatoes and red cabbage and magnificent vanilla ice cream. [...] September 9 [...] [W]as present as the physician at the flogging of eight camp inmates and at one execution by shooting with a small caliber gun."

Grief dallied with nor law nor limit knows. Neither does righteousness. In dance class, Cookie demonstrates a kick to aim at the crotch of a jurist whose name starts with k. Her body a knife ready to defend against those who would kidnap liberty or just plain kill us.

"There is a central channel of subtle energy — a life current — that runs through the core of the body." Cookie doesn't say *kundalini* but shows us how to move it snakelike through and out our bodies, how to ken this energy flowing from temporary partners.

Imagine or find four individuals placed, one at each tip of your k. Make your way along k's pathways to briefly connect with each partner. Like a serpent tasting air, let your body taste the kundalini of each without touch. Rebound from that contact and on to the next, moving each time through the heart of k.

I don't leave class with a plan except to come closer to the bodies of those without houses.

i

Such a harmless-looking individual, narrow body, head spinning. If you're not a danger to self or others, there's no need to restrain you. If you don't need restraint, we've got nothing for you. You're on your own, kid.

Walk a narrow line in inching increments. When you reach a crack, step over it. No need to risk breaking mother's back on top of everything else. Turn tightly on your spot. Step back over crack, return to starting position. Do it again, thinking the whole time: **i** am a person **i** am a very important person **i** am a person of no import. Or stick your fingers in your ears and sing "la la la" to drown out that noise. What happens when someone approaches?

For some, certain interactions Rainer incorporates in *The Concept of Dust* may evoke contact improvisation, which was initiated by Steve Paxton, one of her closest colleagues from Judson Dance Theater days and beyond.[3] It seeks to transcend the limits of the small **i** by turns self-hating and grandiose, by having people play together to create movement. Use the self to go beyond the self, like spiritual systems are designed to do. The book *In Touch,* by psychologist and spiritual teacher John Prendergast, ends with this twelfth-century quote by Chinese Buddhist master Kakuan: "Barefooted and naked of breast, I mingle with the people of the world. My clothes are ragged and dust-laden, and I am ever blissful. I use no magic to extend my life. Now, before me, the dead trees come alive."

i don't think this quote is meant to justify poverty but to show as a goal the self stripped down to the most humble, unguarded, and receptive state. The seeming contradiction of "no magic" and "dead trees come alive" intrigues. If dead trees coming alive isn't magic, what is it? Does humility and a sense of common humanity bring the world into focus in a way that's even better than magic?

i chose the dance class I've been attending precisely because among the offered classes it seemed closest to Rainer's postmodern aesthetic. Contact improv is a strength of both the regular teacher, Christine, and the sub, Cookie, who happens to have taught most of the time **i**'ve been working on this essay. The more contact improv in a given class, the more grins and eye contact. Leaving class, **i** perceive passersby as unconsciously involved in a single, culture-wide dance. What is my capacity to bring the liberated joy **i** feel in class into the polis? What is my means for doing so?

---

3 YVONNE RAINER: I never used or learned or performed Contact Improvisation nor called close body contact in my work by that name —
AUTHOR: The version of this section that Rainer read suggested that she deliberately uses contact improvisation in her work. The section has been revised to indicate that the linking of contact improvisation with Rainer's work is an association that some viewers might make.

p

Paris gardens and zoo provided retired customs officer Henri Rousseau with data points for paintings like "The Sleeping Gypsy." The artwork is wheeled at butoh pace by a pair of professional handlers across the back wall as dancers perform on a sculpture platform turned proscenium in the MoMA performance of *The Concept of Dust.* It was young Rainer's preferred painting. She acknowledges perfect ignorance at that time of the colonialist context in which the work was made. In post-performance conversation, she explains that she was and still is partial to its "strange, lovely fantasy." Her capacity to listen to past personas in a manner both appreciative and analytic creates a palimpsest. "You know, when you make work for so many years, in a way you're always testing what you used to do and being critical of it at the same time. The past carries a kind of baggage that sometimes is useful to me." Originally, Rainer had proposed sleeping under the painting as an offshoot of artist-choreographer Ralph Lemon's series of "Value Talks" at MoMA. Curator Ana Janevski argued Rainer risked being perceived as imitating Tilda Swinton, who had recently slept in one of the museum's glass cases. Rainer parried: she would provide a handout to help problematize the installation. But when she learned that visitors had ogled Swinton, Rainer let go of the concept. Lemon was deeply disappointed but painted a portrait of elder Rainer napping under one of the world's priciest artworks. After seeing the MoMa version of *The Concept of Dust,* he acknowledged that the dance's beauty had expunged his lingering pique.

What remains to be said is devoid of the letter **p**:

> Museums are getting way more adventurous and inclusive in their offerings. But I've yet to hear of any of them functioning as a site of slumber for folks who lack shelter.
>
> I'm trying to balance radiance and shadow, kisses and bruises.
>
> If you want to create your own score for the letter above the above words, my only request is that you do so imagining you're on a stage, in order to stick with my general guidelines in this venture.
>
> "As the body awakens, so does the world."

w

when : will we know : what : the body knows : the body is : "like a huge cathedral : filled with space" : that means every body : is the body : sacred : means sweep : the cathedral : daily lay flowers : at its altar : all : take turns : make these sweeping : gestures : tend : this body we : share

d

There are those for whom postmodern dance never happened. For others the questions it poses are as vital as breath. Yvonne Rainer, a key originator of postmodern dance, has more than anyone invented this method of breathing and helped millions of viewers oxygenate their lungs with it. Yet Rainer herself is allowing elements of modernist and classical dance into her current work. To be sure, *The Concept of Dust* is in many respects a consummately postmodern dance. It begins not with dramatic spectacle but with the dancers milling about in front of the gathering audience, doing warm-ups or chatting. Much of the piece is determined on the spot by the dancers, and there's a disjunction between the texts read aloud and the dancers' phrases. These phrases often do not read as "dancerly": sometimes the dancers, mostly wearing everyday clothes and sneakers, seem to be pausing and thinking about what they might do next; sometimes they play childlike games with each other or engage in quotidian activities such as running or waving. And non-dancers — museum art handlers — move a painting across the space behind the dancers in much the way they would move any painting, albeit at a snail's pace. Much of the time, different dancers are doing different movements that appear to have no overarching coordination. Yet set sections occurring at the beginning, roughly two-thirds of the way through, and at the end provide a shapeliness that hints at narrative. Most of the dance is accompanied by a lush Gavin Bryars composition that addresses the sinking of the *Titanic,* replete with bits of an interview with the oldest living survivor and the tune that was played by the ship's band as the behemoth drowned. All this, followed by intense silence and the dancers' deep gaze into the audience's eyes, provides a sense of journey and emotionally charged arrival or completion, which one associates with more traditionally conceived works. Is Rainer going soft? Maybe so, if soft means allowing whatever she needs to say, to understand, to move, at this moment in her trajectory when, in her parlance, there's nothing left to move.

Today in class I channeled Pina Bausch, my moves expressionistic. Christine, the teacher Cookie's been subbing for, put on a Zoë Keating piece, technicolor cello blossoms. My body leaned into the music, having just passed through the zone of despair between my car and the studio.

Woman seated against a wall. I've had better days, she said, can you slap me up something. Man in a chair, we agreed on the sun. Woman sitting on curb, empty needle held loosely in right hand, body sloped forward and rocking, whimpering softly, left hand pressing nostrils together. Gleaming white SUV inching into the space just next to her.

"Somewhere between conception and birth, inside the womb of your mother, you began to have an embodied sense of living: the feeling of your heart beating, of pressure against your skin, of discomfort and its relief." Right now, the only relief comes from filling each petal with grief.

9

What do you want to relinquish?

The sweaty self-suit, unbreathable fabric, hard-to-reach zipper.

What makes you squirm?

How long it takes. Groping for the zipper.

Why do you squeak?

I squeak against majesty. I squeak for what's silly and small.

Isn't arabesque anachronistic?

All baggage including the cultural kind has its uses. So I listen to the French Suites and weep as I write. Sometimes I get up, move, stretch limbs. Make an awkward arabesque.

m

Regardless of the abuse or neglect we have experienced,

(membranes delicate; reduce possible harms; squirt needle up nose)

(17th and Shotwell, slumps on curb)

(Christine has us lie on backs, arms and legs spread, roll to each curled-up side)

(at Judson, performers looked at each other and the audience)

the core of our being —

(if tissue damaged, passages can't absorb drugs; lengthen time between hits)

(empty needle held, body curved, grey T-shirt drapes bare left shoulder)

(we walk, slow then faster, rotate shoulders, swing arms, pause in any direction)

(they breathed audibly, ran out of breath, sweated, talked things over)

open awareness —

(flush nose; use water ampoules from the exchange — that's what they're designed for)

(rocking, moaning softly, pressing nostrils; white SUV inching in to right)

(plant any body part on floor — magnetizes or repels rest of body into movement)

(the performers began behaving more like human beings)

remains untouched and whole.

V

Begin sitting or standing. Hold your hands up in front of you and spread your fingers wide.

Relax your fingers. Rest them at the outer edges of your clavicle. Draw index tips lightly along the ridge of bone till they meet in the center.

Extend both arms out to your sides. Keep them in the same vertical plane as your torso while lifting them up to a 45-degree angle.

Bring your hands down and clasp them behind your head. Nestle them into the curve of your neck, just below the base of your skull.

Lie down on the floor, arms extending to the sides for ballast. Then lift your straight legs till perpendicular with the floor and spread them wide.

Some bodies learn to lift till balancing on buttocks, arms extended forward from shoulders, torso and straight legs extending up off the floor in opposing directions. This may take practice and should not be done if it would strain your neck or back.

Lie down again. Whatever else you're doing, spread your toes as far from each other as you can.

Locate a partner. Stand next to each other facing the same direction. Hold hands firmly. Slowly lean away from each other, feet planted firmly.

Turn to face your partner, grasp each other's wrists, lean away.

Straighten. Release wrists. Place your hands in front of your heart, prayer position. Flap them open, the base of your palms still touching.

Flatten palms against one another. The lengths of your thumbs pressing against your sternum. Lean toward your partner from the hips. Then straighten up.

Say in a conversational voice, "very, very, very. It was very. We are very. Everything will be very." Say five more times: "very." Let your voice get softer and softer until it is breath.

g

The grass is greener when the sun is yellower. The grass is greener when the sun is yellow.

A body chants these words and makes squeaking noises while dancing a series of slow, quirky poses in the third section of Yvonne Rainer's *Three Satie Spoons.* "I imagine what comes across is incongruity, bizarre — maybe odd or eccentric — although I make no conscious attempts at humor," wrote Rainer in an August 1961 letter, a month after the premier of this, her first solo work, and fifty-four years before the premier of *The Concept of Dust.* "My image sometimes takes the form of a disoriented body in which one part doesn't know what the other part is doing."

The majority of houseless individuals I observe are highly organized, directed people who appear to manage phenomenally well in nightmare conditions. Some portion resemble Rainer in that dance. Many housed people do too. Yet there are reasons you're more likely to see bizarre behavior outside than inside. There aren't enough mental health services, addiction programs. There aren't enough safe, comfortable places to get a good night's sleep. As we're all aware after Abu Ghraib, sleep deprivation leads to hallucinations and psychosis.

A score: find and watch a video of choreographer Sally Silvers performing this dance as taught to her by Rainer. Teach it to yourself, modifying to match your capacity. Strive, but do not hold out for perfection. Perform the piece at the intersection of 17th and Shotwell Streets in San Francisco, sound equipment blaring music by Erik Satie. Have a friend hand out slips of paper crediting Rainer; have another gather responses.

She's probably connected to that dance school down the block.

Pretty sure I've seen her before. I think she lives here, at the corner.

Why are these movements and sounds affecting me so? I was just walking by. Now I feel ____.

"When we are attuned and congruent with our deepest nature, the chronic inner grip of tension uncoils," writes Prendergast. Rainer experienced this at her premier. "I have one bad moment of absolute dread — my heart is like an inert stone, a feeling of paralysis. Then the stage lights fade up; I face them, a vague sea of spectacles — the lights protect me — I feel life and energy flowing back. My music begins and I am transported into a very special world. I felt beautiful, confident, knowing, proud, completely carried away by the magic of my own gestures and movements."

Thank your responders. But refuse to budge from the puzzling intersection of dance and houselessness.[4]

---

4 YVONNE RAINER: Did you really perform that piece on the corner of 17th and Shotwell, displacing the homeless woman?!!
AUTHOR: No, this was an imaginary score.

h

Easy to fall into judgment. This person is classist, that person is classist, all the classes are classist, the business class has published a report recommending a regional approach, are these the people to take the lead in solving the problem, business means profit lines pockets it's up to each to grab and grub, meritocratic myth that those without are to blame, the report reports Bay Area residents rank homelessness the third biggest problem after housing affordability and traffic congestion, sitting in a jam worse than tens of thousands having no home, I hand out indictments daily blur gaze away from humans holding signs because what would happen if I gave to this person whose history I don't know and don't understand, what if they use those bucks to buy substances not for me to decide please stop revisiting this at 7 in the morning 4 in the afternoon racing to manage Monday Tuesday Friday can't dilate to see my problems are someone else's ice cream sundae with a cherry on top, refuse to inhabit person outside window holding sign saying Down on My Luck Anything Helps stepping between exhaust-exuding cars, eye contact means obligation, if I give now what about tomorrow stewing in my own little heartache machine carries me amidst 28,000-plus living without safety or comfort more than the population of half the 101 cities comprising the greater Bay Area with its cutting edge culture where the therapist yoga instructor museum exhibit support me in continuing to heal PTSD lingering from childhood in muscles posture amygdala hijacks per day keep practicing a different tune goes something like "revisit your original limiting belief," heal, go way beyond healing make art, innovate, hold your own, your own hand write about those cool postmodern dancer women who broke out enlarged our world whether we know it or not whether we see art frees or at least documents our world today study dance rekindle kinetic gestures enter words reach to cells in reader's body but can barely drag self to page after a week of hustling late to identify what the Buddhists call right livelihood while also taking all invitations to join the creativity party because I'm late no offspring so art will have to pass on my whatever while also trying to stay in relation to peers elders youngers who might visit my old folks' home now and then give and take sponging in the jangled energy fall flat on couch for hours the Buddhists drone gently in my ear does this sound like one long excuse or an attempt to tease out the tangle in my heart each time I pass a houseless person for whom my troubles an ice cream sundae for someone on whom the cold rain pours hot sun beats others sniff at prey on or just plain ignore someone dragging their stuff in a cart blocking doorway makes a bad bed will you feel lucky if you get placed in a so-called cabin community in Oakland a so-called tiny home in San Jose the latest attempts to get folks off the streets off the banks of Lake Merritt where they pose an inconvenience for picnickers what if you do get some kind of housing and hate your roommate feel as some do this is a new form of prison people are pouring themselves into solving this crisis has complicated roots but we can certainly say continues to be served by a meritocratic myth that still has me in its clutches clambering up the ladder to perfect freedom of thought and action toward success don't knock feminist ambition but does it compensate for early deficits does it fend off primal fear of being banished from the community better to practice falling down and getting back up falling down and getting back up falling down and rolling around keeping core low to the ground like dance teacher Christine says from that center leap out connect I'm saying let's take that outside the studio don't know how but that's my platform that's what I'm standing on what I'm running on running to I'm running I'm creeping I'm whimpering I'm weeping I'm laughing I'm hunching I'm mincing I'm dancing all the way over to you

u

struggle to

untie knots unintentionally

tangled

sing strangled

torn and buffeted

brink unblanketed

unrested

resist unwarranted

arrest, refuse

uncivil rules

u are not dust

till dusk

when all fall

down

C

Cleave: what dance or any art does, slice through what separates us so we

Can: recognize other

Citizens: a series of them in a video responds to the question, how could the

City: compensate you for what it's stolen via official sweeps; the answer is

Can't: put a dollar value on pictures of mother carried in pack for years

Cecil and Janice: have said look at the person, don't walk by, everything follows from that

Crux: that Jesus, this humanitarian

Crisis: not one big flash but slow wave picking up more and more humans,

Caging us: system logic

Cultivates: some qualities over others, war, what is it good for absolutely nothing except

Caveat: making billions of dollars, system logic for

Chaos: destroying people born and raised in Aleppo or San Francisco, displaced then shot by

Cops: but

Current: structures have plenty of fissures, not

Complete: and not total, revolution is what we make in the interstices, where hope lives

a, t, n, s (retrospective)

The Concept of Dust is an artist's own retrospective as she approaches the end. She samples dance phrases she's created over decades, phrases that themselves were sampled from various sources, some for example evoking silent films, Charlie Chaplin or Buster Keaton perhaps; she counts both among her influences.

Disconnections multiply in this piece. The dance phrases, some of which appear at designated points and others which dancers may initiate at will but according to predetermined constraints, form a jagged collage. Atop that collage awkwardly perch other elements: art handlers moving a painting across the back of the space; a piano tuner tuning a piano and then playing a piece on it; a musical score by Gavin Bryars which is its own collage, folding fragments of recorded speech and various tunes and sound effects into a slowed-down rendering of a hymn. As if all that isn't enough of a jumble, yet another collage teeters on this scrap heap of variables, comprising excerpts from various texts that Rainer and the dancers read aloud. Some of these texts began life as sound bites: "I've been to hell and back and it was wonderful" is adapted from a phrase the artist Louise Bourgeois embroidered on a handkerchief in 1996. Some Rainer excerpted from longer works, such as a quote from an unfinished essay arguing that war reveals the true nature of nation states, by early twentieth-century pacifist writer Randolph Bourne. Some can be easily tracked down online while others are more elusive. Passages about the early Islamic empire were copied, it turns out, from the Metropolitan Museum of Art wall plaques. And who knows where Rainer came across the transcription of a dream about the dreamer's body being sawed to pieces, from which the dreamer wakes thinking, "I am a danger to myself."

In the 2015 MoMA performance, the awkwardness is heightened as Rainer roams around onstage with a sheaf of papers and a handheld mic, thrusting the latter in dancers' faces when it's their turn to read. She sometimes has to chase after them or stand around waiting till they are in a position to be able to read text. She has to freeze mid-sentence to turn a page. She drops a page. She and the readers struggle at times to pronounce Arabic terms. One dancer misreads a phrase and apologizes.

Yet out of all this alienation and awkwardness blossoms beauty. The slow-moving, solemn musical score by Bryars unifies all the disparate pieces, but it's not just that. These dance phrases, textual fragments, and other elements suture themselves into a vast, wild quilt, one that includes communication and confusion, intimate moments and international crises, comedy and violence, the ancient past and the twenty-first century, life on Earth and the workings of the cosmos.

There are artists who lead with their hearts, those who lead with their bodies, and those who lead with their minds. I think of Rainer as inhabiting the last category. But all art worth its salt makes a home for the full experience of being human. When I watch this piece over and over, attending to each small fragment of gesture and word, working to find relation and allow disconnection, I feel like I'm on a crowded city street in an altered state, one that allows me to open myself to the panoply, the cacophony, the catastrophe that is us now. Us at the front end of a trail of time that stretches back and back, us on our little pinhead Earth in space that stretches into infinity.

I said retrospective but I meant requiem. Bryars's piece is called "The Sinking of the Titanic." An elder woman's voice threads through the music, testimony of the last survivor. An artist in her 80s who's been making uncompromising work for most of her life can say whatever the hell she wants. Facing death she can say, We're that ship. We might be that ship. I might be that woman.[5]

Maybe she just liked the sound of that score. Maybe that's what I'll say to myself at 3 a.m. so I can get some sleep. What will you say in your own bed?

Do you have a bed?

Do you have a house?

Houselessness entered this piece with Amy, a woman I noticed inhabiting the corner of 17th and Shotwell in San Francisco's Mission District, where I've been attending dance classes out of a desire to get closer to postmodern dance, enter into it with my whole body, not just with words. The dancer-choreographers whose work I've been studying broke so many barriers erected by Martha Graham and other modern dance giants. They took performance off its pedestal, embracing notions of ordinariness. They used "found" gestures from domestic and street life, wore everyday clothing, and performed in nontraditional venues, including, at times, city streets. The dance class I've been taking and the dancers who teach and take the class operate in the same sphere — the ideas that Rainer and her ilk introduced, radical in their time, are now commonplace. My classmates show up wearing anything, run through the space like joggers and jaguars, stop abruptly, facing every which way, to waggle a dancy downward dog. Filled up to my eyeballs with this lexicon of fluidity and inclusion, I found myself noticing bodies both inside and outside the studio. Leaving class, I lifted the gaze I've learned over years to cast down or up or anywhere away from the ocean of suffering. I slowed my pace, turned toward bodies and faces of houseless individuals.

I started recognizing individuals as I came and went. One woman in particular magnetized me, so reliably present at the corner, seated on the curb, standing still, or pacing. I'm not the first to notice her. No sooner did I say "woman at the corner of 17th and Shotwell" than an acquaintance responded: "I know exactly who you're talking about. She's always standing there, alone. Being a male I wouldn't want to invade her space, but I always wonder, who is this person, what is her story? She seems so vulnerable yet so rooted. She's a force field at that intersection."

After crossing her path for a few weeks, I decided to approach. I didn't want to feel like I was just spying, using her. I wanted to put myself on the line, person to person. I attempted to strike up a conversation, but she was some unknowable combination of unwilling and unable to engage with me. Maybe someone more graceful or skilled than I could have gotten farther,

---

5 YVONNE RAINER: Love the descriptions of *The Concept of Dust* —

incurred greater trust. Or maybe that someone would have sensed beforehand how futile engagement would prove. I'm only me, and she's only she. Besides the substances I've seen her inject, who knows what other traumas and illnesses she's grappling with.

I went home and hunted through all my toiletries and food, looking for small, light, flat gifts. I called a trusted advisor. He said, don't give her things right now. I thought, as I've thought so many times after receiving wise counsel, thank you for saving me from myself.

I had wanted to focus on one person because that's what I felt I could handle. And now, what could I do but use this failed communication as the next portal to move through.

I saw all the bodies — those of the fit, well-dressed people snacking at the corner café, strolling down the sidewalk, entering lovely refurbished Victorians and spanking-new lofts, and the suffering, destitute people occupying the same arena — as part of a complex dance. A gripping performance anyone can observe, on a particular street corner in a particular city. Itself a mere dot on a world stage on which is playing out the ever greater divide. The dance appears improvised: a life went off track, a corner has a confluence. Such framing soothes. Yet I say nothing that hasn't been said better by others, when I say that deep structures make the mushrooming catastrophe all but inevitable. Beneath the navigation of bodies across intersections, through gates, up and down ladders, bedrock beliefs in individual freedom allow us to attribute accrual of wealth to resourcefulness and strength, dismiss poverty and despair as signs of laziness and weakness. Our government sanctions this view. Yet among the housed and well fed, some part of us knows, however hard we try to shut out the information, that more and more people are falling into the chasm. And the anxiety this creates leads us to suck even harder on our iced matcha green tea and stare even more fixedly into our iPhone XYZ. We need this, we need to enjoy ourselves on this all too short weekend because we work hard to pay the rent, to pay the mortgage, to afford this tea, this phone, this good time we're having. We work hard at the job, the gym, the diet, the smile, the lingo, the logo, the spreadsheet, the setup, the debrief, we work hard. And this is our break, so please don't ruin it.

Here is a dance score: You are a person caught in a sticky web. You struggle and struggle to get out. The harder you wriggle and flail, the more bound your limbs become.

I can learn about the housing crisis, the opioid crisis, the education crisis, the unlivable-wage crisis, the overcrowded-prisons crisis, the hunger crisis, the health crisis. Each time I look into one of these crises, I find visionary, smart, resourceful people working as hard as they can to solve it. And I also find a whole lot of greed. Across so many of these vectors, someone's getting rich, healthy, and happy off someone else getting poor, sick, and depressed. Is this system working, even for the well-off? Emphatically yes, and also, maybe, no, right? How free are you when you have to bury your gaze in your latte or your phone and scurry past your fellow humans with their tent or cart or bag or nothing but the clothes on their backs, because it's looking like spider or fly out here and I'm going to make damned sure I'm the spider.

These days I'm talking to myself like this.

I'm dancing this score.

I'm trying to wake up, to use a favorite metaphor of the spirituality teachers.

And as I turn to spiritual texts for guidance, besides the image of waking up I'm struck by the preponderance of the word "home" to describe spiritual arrival. Like the inspiring John Prendergast, whom I quoted earlier: "The more we take ourselves and others to be objects, the further away from home we are." I used the word as a metaphor myself just a few paragraphs ago: "all art worth its salt makes a home for the full experience of being human."

Score: Every time you hear the word "home" used metaphorically or literally, come to a dead halt. Meditate in complete stillness, right there on the spot, about how deeply our language takes for granted that every one of us wants, needs, and deserves a home. Let this awareness permeate you — mind and heart, torso and limbs. When you move again, move from that knowledge.

This is how I'm talking to myself.

I'm dancing this score.[6]

---

6 YVONNE RAINER: Powerful articulation of the "plight" of us middle-class progressives — Do you at least vote?
AUTHOR: Yes! And more!

Notes

r

"From the age of twelve ..." is from Rainer (2006, 108).

"Learn the latter from Rainer, whose dance *The Concept of Dust* ...": This essay discusses the June 13, 2015 MoMA performance of Yvonne Rainer's dance *The Concept of Dust, or How Do You Look When There's Nothing Left to Move?* Since that performance, the piece has been retitled *The Concept of Dust: Continuous Project — Altered Annually*, and, as the new subtitle suggests, continues to evolve.

"We try to hold ..." is from Prendergast (2015, 103).

o

"When I first dropped into it ..." is from Prendergast (2015, 165).

"The readings appear ..." is from an observation by Rainer during a conversation between Yvonnne Rainer, Douglas Crimp, and MoMA Associate Curator Ana Janevski following the June 2015 performance of *The Concept of Dust* (The Museum of Modern Art 2015a).

"Anyone in the group ..." is from an impromptu contribution by dancer Pat Catterson to the post-performance conversation of *The Concept of Dust* (The Museum of Modern Art 2015a).

b

"Rainer's choreography ..." is from Wood (2007, 9–11).

"Take a few deep breaths ..." is from Prendergast (2015, 161).

e

"Beckett said ..." is from an observation Lyn Tillman texted to Ana Janevski, who read it aloud during the *The Concept of Dust* post-performance conversation (The Museum of Modern Art 2015a).

"marvelous error" is from the poem "Last Night as I Was Sleeping," by Antonio Machado, quoted in Prendergast (2015, 48).

"The invisible ..." is from Schulz (2015). It is part of a longer passage from the essay read aloud by Rainer during *The Concept of Dust*.

j

"Random structure ..." and "dark and pessimistic" are from an observation by Rainer during *The Concept of Dust* post-performance conversation (The Museum of Modern Art 2015a).

"Wounds to the heart ..." is from Prendergast (2015, 149).

f

"We may call it ..." is from Prendergast (2015, 187).

x

"Nobody wants ..." is from the poem "One Crossed Out" (Howe 1997, 53).

"Only labor cares ..." is from the poem "Plutocracy" (Howe 1997, 19).

"I ran the risk ..." is from an observation by Rainer during *The Concept of Dust* post-performance conversation (The Museum of Modern Art 2015a).

"The more we take ourselves ..." is from Prendergast (2015, 185).

y

"As Cunningham always said ..." is from an observation by Rainer during a 2011 conversation with Sally Banes as part of the Talking Dance interview series at the Walker Art Center in Minneapolis, Minnesota (Walker Art Center 2011).

"I studied with Merce ..." is from an observation by Rainer during a 2012 conversation with David Velasco, part of a series titled "Judson at 50," published in *Art Forum* (Rainer 2012).

"beehive / here inside my heart" and "white combs / and sweet honey / from my old failures" are from the poem "Last Night as I Was Sleeping," by Antonio Machado, quoted in Prendergast (2015, 48).

l

"So I find I can still ..." is from an observation by Rainer during *The Concept of Dust* post-performance conversation (The Museum of Modern Art 2015a).

"made no effort ..." is from an observation by Rainer, quoted in Lambert-Beatty (2008, 141).

"pretty tyrannical dictator" is from an observation by Rainer, quoted in Wood (2007, 28).

"I'm not as democratic ..." and "No" are statements by Rainer during *The Concept of Dust* post-performance conversation (The Museum of Modern Art 2015a).

"They keep ..." is from an observation by Rainer during *The Concept of Dust* post-performance conversation (The Museum of Modern Art 2015a).

"Consider how you subtly ..." is from Prendergast (2015, 103).

z

"We started with ...," "We rolled ...," "Groups of five ...," and "Across 15th Street ..." are from notes I took after a dance class at ODC Dance Commons in San Francisco on January 13, 2019.

"Clearly, there is ..." is from Prendergast (2015, 37).

"What has happened ..." is from an observation by Rainer during *The Concept of Dust* post-performance conversation (The Museum of Modern Art 2015a).

k

"'Tis double death ...," "He ten times pines ...," "To see the salve ...," and "Grief dallied with ..." are from *The Rape of Lucrece* in Shakespeare (1911, 1261–83).

"in the heart of the San Francisco Mission" is from the website for Robin's Café, http://www.robinscafesf.com.

"September 6, 1942 ..." is from the diary of a Nazi doctor, read aloud by Rainer during *The Concept of Dust* (The Museum of Modern Art 2015b).

"There is a central channel ..." is from Prendergast (2015, 39).

i

"contact improvisation, which was initiated by Steve Paxton ..." is documented in sources such as the journal *Contact Quarterly* (2022).

"Barefooted and naked of breast ..." is quoted on page 191 of Prendergast (2015).

p

The information about Henri Rousseau using his familiarity with Paris's gardens and zoo to paint works such as "Sleeping Gypsy" is from *Modernism* (48), by Robin Walz.

"strange, lovely fantasy" is from an observation by Rainer during *The Concept of Dust* post-performance conversation (The Museum of Modern Art 2015a).

"You know, when you make work ..." is an observation by Rainer in Rainer (2015b).

Rainer writes about her foiled plan to sleep under "The Sleeping Gypsy" in the magazine *Triple Canopy*. The piece includes the printed statement she had intended to distribute to museum visitors and an image of the painting by Ralph Lemon (Rainer 2015a).

"As the body awakens ..." is from Prendergast (2015, 190).

w

"like a huge cathedral filled with space" is from Prendergast (2015, 162).

d

"Somewhere between conception and birth ..." is from the foreword to Prendergast (2015, ix), by psychologist and meditation teacher Rick Hanson.

q

"The sweaty self-suit, unbreathable fabric, hard-to-reach zipper" takes off from this passage from Prendergast (2015, 81): "As long as we maintain a separate sense of self, we will carry some degree of the belief that we are lacking or flawed. It is the inevitable baggage of the 'little me.'"

"All baggage including the cultural kind ..." takes off from the above-referenced passage in Prendergast (2015) as well as Yvonne Rainer's observations about the "baggage" she makes use of in her work. In her conversation with Charles Aubin in *Performa* magazine she said, "You know, when you make work for so many years, in a way you're always testing what you used to do and being critical of it at the same time. The past carries a kind of baggage that sometimes is useful to me. I call it 'raiding my icebox.' It means going into your closet of old knickknacks and discovering little things that have new potential" (Rainer 2015b). In a conversation with RoseLee Goldberg in *Document* journal she said, "So coming back to dance and the way I operate now, there's all this baggage I'm carrying around; my work now is full of very early dance moves" (Rainer 2017).

m

The language about injecting drugs nasally with minimal harm is drawn from a slide presentation by Terry Morris, coordinator of the San Francisco AIDS Foundation's Speed Project, at the 9th National Harm Reduction Conference in Portland, Oregon, in November 2012, hosted by the Harm Reduction Coalition.

Some of the language in "m" is excerpted from an observation by Trisha Brown in a 1978 interview: "At Judson, the performers looked at each other and the audience, they breathed audibly, ran out of breath, sweated, talked things over. They began behaving more like human beings, revealing what was thought of as deficiencies as well as their skills" (Brown 1978).

"Regardless of the abuse or neglect we have experienced, the core of our being — open awareness — remains untouched and whole" is from Prendergast (2015, 125).

The section includes notes I took after a dance class at ODC Dance Commons in San Francisco, CA, on April 7, 2019.

v

This section is based loosely on a passage in Prendergast (2015, 124–25).

"Locate a partner. Stand next to each other facing the same direction. Hold hands firmly. Slowly lean away from each other, feet planted firmly" replicates a dance phrase in the "final tableaux" section of *The Concept of Dust.*

g

"I imagine what comes across …" and "My image sometimes …" are from Rainer (2006, 204).

The information about the effects of sleep deprivation is drawn from Waters et al. (2018).

"A score: find and watch …" refers to a video of Sally Silvers dancing *Three Satie Spoons* that was projected during a videotaped interview of Rainer by Sally Banes (Walker Art Center 2011).

"When we are attuned …" is from Prendergast (2015, 107).

"I have one bad moment …" is from Rainer (2006, 210).

h

"the business class has published ..." refers to a report by the Bay Area Council Economic Institute (2019) titled *Bay Area Homelessness: A Regional View of a Regional Crisis.*

"revisit your original limiting belief" is from Prendergast (2015, 86).

"will you feel lucky ..." draws on news coverage of the houseless community's mixed response to recent government initiatives to provide shelter, for example, Kendall (2018).

u

This section draws in part on the phrase "many may never have had a fully in-the-body experience" in Prendergast (2015, 60).

c

This section is shaped by a conversation with Rob Avila, on the morning of May 26, 2019 at a café near 24th and Folsom where poor and rich people crisscrossed in morning sun and many cops milled, prior to the Carnival parade. So many cops, relaxed, sipping coffee and chatting, yet ever vigilant, on duty as they say, armed bodies encased in the bulletproof blue of potential menace. Rob is a writer-thinker-activist who works at the intersection of art and politics; for several years he was immersed in the houselessness crisis as a staff member at Glide Church. What I wrote for **c** is based on and inspired by his responses to my questions.

"a series of them in a video" refers to the Stolen Belonging project, https://www.stolenbelonging.org/project, which documents the impact on houseless people of having their belongings confiscated during sweeps conducted in San Francisco.

"Cecil and Janice" are Cecil Williams and Janice Mirikitani, founders of Glide Church in San Francisco.

a, t, n, s (retrospective)

The reference to Rainer's sampling of dance phrases she created earlier in her career is drawn from an observation by Rainer during *The Concept of Dust* post-performance conversation (The Museum of Modern Art 2015a).

The phrase Louise Bourgeois embroidered on a handkerchief was "I have been to hell and back and let me tell you it was wonderful," according to Pomeroy (2010).

The quote by Randolph Bourne that Rainer uses is from Young (2015, 340): "Wartime brings the ideal of the State out into very clear relief and reveals attitudes and tendencies that were hidden. In times of peace the sense of the State flags in a Republic that is not militarized. For war is essentially the health of the State."

The reference to Rainer using information about the early Islamic empire that she copied from wall plaques at the Metropolitan Museum of Art is drawn from an observation by Rainer during *The Concept of Dust* post-performance conversation (The Museum of Modern Art 2015a).

"The more we take ourselves ..." is from Prendergast (2015, 185).

Afterword

Ralph Lemon

Attending to the Thing (Itself)

> "[The untidy child] hunts the spirits whose trace [s]he scents in things; between spirits and things years are passed in which [her] field of vision remains free of people. [Her] life is like a dream: [s]he knows nothing lasting." —Walter Benjamin (1997, 73)

I'm embarrassed to say this, but I didn't see Simone Forti's work live until 2012, at St. Mark's Danspace Project. *News Animations.* Part of *Judson NOW.* The beginning of the 50-year anniversary of the Judson Dance Theater, and the many things proposed by that. How much of the force of Simone's 1960 *Dance Constructions* helped usher in that Dance Theater. Watching Simone for the first time, 52 years after that dance-world earthquake, I felt a strange calm. As though something in my many years of performance-watching was missing something that I hadn't known wasn't there, and this moment was beginning to fill in that big empty space. I saw Simone again at MoMA: her solo, *King's Fool,* another part of *News Animations* (2013). And *illlummminnnatttionnnsssss!!!!!!!* (2014) with Charlemagne Palestine, a duet. And more recently, *Simone Forti With Obstructions by Robert Morris* (2018), at the Castelli Gallery. Being in the presence of Simone and her work has become a pilgrimage for me.

Simone dances like an untidy child, one who is completely present. I have a 10-year-old daughter at home. She dances every day. Her movement body is brand new every single time. Its purpose and efficiency. Simone has danced like that every single time, I imagine. But Simone's every single time, a modern mode I have witnessed, possesses a deeply wise gravitas, a history, with no hierarchy. Simone's materials are her dancing, writing, talking, and interactions with objects, any objects, it seems. The whole is a phenomenal daily practice. Life. There are so many ways to see Simone, her work. She makes art look easy. And profound. As she guides her multivalent practice to its ultimate and generative disappearing. Maybe all that I've missed of this long radical passage doesn't really matter, because what I witness now is sublime and vaporous.

And Present Still

Yvonne Rainer walked out of a performance of mine, *Scaffold Room* (2015), at the Kitchen. She later emailed me, "Ralph, I had to leave when she [April Matthis] lay down upstage and the shrieking began. My ears couldn't take it. You test us, Ralph. You test us."

Dear Yvonne, word has it that there was a lot of screaming going on in the '60s, your '60s. At Yoko Ono's loft in 1961, in Simone Forti's *Rollers*, "the single tone shouting, full out!" And your screaming fit in your own *Three Seascapes* (1962). Your own radical shrieking. I have had very good teachers, Yvonne.

I saw Yvonne's performance work live for the first time in *Past Forward* (2001) at Brooklyn Art Museum (BAM). When and where Yvonne returned to dance after making movies and teaching. She made a collage of her old work, *After Many a Summer Dies the Swan* (2002). I remember it was like watching something historically and conspicuously famous, known but not recognized. I thought that there was absolutely nothing pedestrian or ordinary about *Trio A* (1966). Another earthquake. How artful and artless it was at 35 years old. I also remember thinking how fresh, contemporary Yvonne's physical body seemed, its present-ness, especially in Steve Paxton's *Satisfyin' Lover* (1967). Just her walking. Just that. Her walking held information, an agentic simplicity that no other walking body on that stage had, or could imagine.

Fast forward to *The Concept of Dust* (2015). MoMA. My favorite Yvonne Rainer work, of my generational watching. I mostly recall being in awe of all the dancers, my friends, my generation, their dynamic histories exploding their dancing. And Yvonne's almost 80-year-old body framing them, a performance fully present, walking, again, and talking, reading, again. Her unreliable performance rants, her elegant rage. How comforting. A body seeming to weep this time, a glorious weeping, her body's historical urgency. Joy.

Simone also had work, *Past Forward: Scramble and Huddle*, in the lobby at BAM in 2001, but I didn't see it. I saw a version of *Huddle* much later on a DVD from a 2004 performance in LA. I have seen many live versions since. I adore the way *Huddle* begins, the alive preparation, the nothing-but-a-huddle, before anything happens. It says everything.

Back to Joy

I wondered if these next few sentences should be part of this afterword. But here they are, my excerpted thoughts on the nothing-but-a-huddle of Simone, Yvonne, and Steve Paxton in *Tea for Three* (2017), at St. Mark's Danspace Project. A little more of almost everything I wish to share with Sarah and Valerie, the authors of this book. Billed as a "dance and performance conversation," it was remarkable in how unremarkable it was. Inconspicuous. I remember being there but don't remember very much of what they were actually doing, other than Simone's sublime and unaffected physical curiosity, Yvonne's bold and persistent attempts at making up (magical) structures, and Steve's adamant and resonating quiet. Three very different doings, negotiated play in the space, the spirited conversation of three long-time artists and friends. It doesn't matter that I don't remember more. The emphatically embodied histories each of them brought to that space and time was enough to pay close attention to. The art part collapsing. They and we were there: I remember that and that is more than enough.

Simone and Yvonne. Their present and historical bodies inspire me. Their different mythologies, imagined and otherwise, their different corporeal performance practices, rhythms. Genius. Their bodies are still vitally, vigilantly in front of me (even when they're not). They work on stuff with a devotion seemingly infinite. I care about this brilliant and untidy generosity; I care about how deeply they care about what it is that they do and have done. And how I get to witness it, not just read about it or imagine it. And how they keep doing it, finding more to do, until there is (inevitably) no more. The no more, no doubt, becoming its own vital thing. A grand lesson in how to get to the best art labor. Life. Thank you, Simone. Thank you, Yvonne.

Bibliography

Adorno, Theodor W. 1991. "The Essay as Form." In *Notes to Literature: Volume One*, edited by Rolf Tiedemann, translated by Shierry Weber Nicholson. Columbia University Press.

Arlen, Harold. 1939. "The Merry Old Land of Oz." In *The Wizard of Oz*, directed by Vincent Fleming. Metro-Goldwyn-Mayer.

Banes, Sally. 1987. *Terpsichore in Sneakers: Post-Modern Dance*. Wesleyan University Press.

———. 1993. *Democracy's Body: Judson Dance Theater, 1962–1964*. Duke University Press.

Bay Area Council Economic Institute. 2019. *Bay Area Homelessness: A Regional View of a Regional Crisis*. April. http://www.bayareaeconomy.org/files/pdf/Homelessness_Report_2019_web.pdf.

Bender, Shawn. 2012. *Taiko Boom: Japanese Drumming in Place and Motion*. University of California Press.

Benjamin, Walter. 1997. *One Way Street and Other Writings*. Translated by Edmund Jephcott and Kingsley Shorter. Verso.

Bennahum, Ninotchka, Wendy Perron, and Bruce Robertson, eds. 2017. *Radical Bodies: Anna Halprin, Simone Forti, and Yvonne Rainer in California and New York, 1955–1972*. University of California Press.

Bossiere, Zoë, and Erica Trabold. 2023. "The Lyric Essay as Resistance: An Interview with Zoë Bossiere and Erica Trabold." Interview by Laura Laing. *Brevity Blog*, March 22. https://brevity.wordpress.com/2023/03/22/the-lyric-essay-as-resistance.

Brown, Angela. 2017. "'Radical Juxtapositions': Adam Pendleton and Yvonne Rainer in an Exchange of Memory and Motion." *ARTNews*, January 11. https://www.artnews.com/art-news/artists/radical-juxtapositions-adam-pendleton-and-yvonne-rainer-in-an-exchange-of-memory-and-motion-7582.

Brown, Trisha. 1978. "Trisha Brown: An Interview." Interview by Anne Livet. In *Contemporary Dance: An Anthology of Lectures, Interviews and Essays with Many of the Most Important Contemporary American Choreographers, Scholars and Critics*, edited by Anne Livet. Abbeville.

Bryan-Wilson, Julia. 2012. "Practicing *Trio A*." *October* 140: 54–74. DOI: 10.1162/OCTO_a_00089.

———. 2015. "Simone Forti Goes to the Zoo." *October* 152: 26–52. DOI: 10.1162/OCTO_a_00215.

Burt, Ramsay. 2006. *Judson Dance Theater: Performative Traces*. Routledge.

Cavarero, Adriana. 2005. *For More Than One Voice: Toward a Philosophy of Vocal Expression.* Translated by Paul A. Kottman. Stanford University Press.

Chan, Erin. 2002. "Taiko, Where Women Pound Out Empowerment." *The Seattle Times,* August 14. https://archive.seattletimes.com/archive/20020814/wdrummers14/taiko-where-women-pound-out-empowerment.

Chaucer, Geoffrey. n.d. "An ABC (The Prayer of Our Lady)." *Poets.org.* https://poets.org/poem/abc-prayer-our-lady.

Cheng, Jennifer S., April Freely, Shamala Gallagher, Aisha Sabatini Sloan, and Addie Tsai. 2018. "The Lyric Essay's Ghosts and Shadows: A Conversation." *Essay Daily,* March 12. https://www.essaydaily.org/2018/03/jennifer-s-cheng-april-freely-shamala.html.

Cole, Norma. 2009. "Worldstruck, with an Instrument." Interview by Robin Tremblay-McGaw. *X Poetics,* March 4. http://xpoetics.blogspot.com/2009/03/worldstruck-with-instrument.html.

Contact Quarterly: Dance and Improvisation Journal. 2022. "About Contact Improvisation (CI)." https://contactquarterly.com/contact-improvisation/about.

Cooper, Michael. 2017. "Rehearse, Ice Feet, Repeat: The Life of a New York City Ballet Corps Dancer." *The New York Times,* January 26. https://www.nytimes.com/2017/01/26/arts/dance/rehearse-ice-feet-repeat-the-life-of-a-new-york-city-ballet-corps-dancer.html.

Crawford, Jack. 2020. "Running in Sneakers, the Judson Dance Theater." *Smarthistory,* September 12. https://smarthistory.org/judson-dance-theater.

Elephant Nature Park. n.d. "Interesting and Fascinating Facts about Elephants' Feet and Legs." https://www.elephantnaturepark.org/interesting-and-fascinating-facts-about-elephants-feet-and-legs.

Enkamp, Jesse. n.d. "What Every Karate-ka Should Know About 'Kiai!'" *Karate by Jesse.* https://www.karatebyjesse.com/kiai-scream-meaning-purpose-why.

Film at Lincoln Center. 2017. "Film Society Talks | Yvonne Rainer and Lynne Tillman." *YouTube,* August 9. https://www.youtube.com/watch?v=eT4OmIKSTPk.

Fischer, Josh. 2018. "Choreography in a Diner: Adam Pendleton's Meeting with Yvonne Rainer." *Big Red and Shiny,* February 6. https://bigredandshiny.org/38492/choreography-in-a-diner-adam-pendletons-meeting-with-yvonne-rainer.

Fleischmann, T. Clutch. 2013. "Ill-Fit the World." In *Bending Genre: Essays on Creative Nonfiction,* edited by Margot Singer and Nicole Walker. Bloomsbury.

Fondation PHI. 2016. "Simone Forti: News Animations | Performance et causerie | Affinités | DHC/ART | 2016." *Vimeo,* June 29. https://vimeo.com/172744953.

Fondazione Furla. 2017. "Furla Series #01: Simone Forti: To Play the Flute." http://www.fondazionefurla.org/furla-series-event/simone-forti-to-play-the-flute.

Forti, Simone. 1998. *Handbook in Motion: An Account of an Ongoing Personal Discourse and Its Manifestations in Dance.* Published by author.

———. 2010. "Simone Forti with Claudia La Rocco." Interview by Claudia La Rocco. *The Brooklyn Rail,* April. https://brooklynrail.org/2010/04/dance/simone-forti-with-claudia-la-rocco.

———. 2015. "Interview with Simone Forti." Interview by Alessandra Nicifero. *Robert Rauschenberg Foundation.* https://www.rauschenbergfoundation.org/artist/oral-history/simone-forti.

———. 2018a. "Simone Forti in Conversation with Jennie Goldstein." Interview by Jennie Goldstein. *Movement Research,* October 18. https://movementresearch.org/publications/critical-correspondence/simone-forti-in-conversation-with-jennie-goldstein-1.

———. 2018b. "Sound Tracks: An Interview with Simone Forti." Interview by Barbara Browning. *The Paris Review,* May 4. https://www.theparisreview.org/blog/2018/05/04/sound-tracks-an-interview-with-simone-forti.

Foundation for Contemporary Arts. n.d. "Yvonne Rainer." https://www.foundationforcontemporaryarts.org/recipients/yvonne-rainer.

Gladman, Renee. 2016. *Calamities.* Wave Books.

Gotta Dance: Fun. Fit. Focus. 2021. "Brief History of Jazz Dance." March 31. https://gotta-dance.com/brief-history-of-jazz-dance.

Guadagnino, Kate. 2019. "The Pioneers of Postmodern Dance, 60 Years Later." *The New York Times Style Magazine,* March 20. https://www.nytimes.com/2019/03/20/t-magazine/postmodern-dance.html.

Heaney, Scott. n.d. "What Is 'Kiai'?" *The Martial Way.* http://the-martial-way.com/what-is-kiai.

Hermes, Will. 2000. "The Story of '4'33"'." *NPR,* May 8. https://www.npr.org/2000/05/08/1073885/4-33.

Howe, Fanny. 1997. *One Crossed Out.* Graywolf Press.

Jarman-Ivens, Freya. 2011. *Queer Voices: Technologies, Vocalities, and the Musical Flaw.* Palgrave Macmillan.

Josephs, Susan, 2009. "Yvonne Rainer Is in Her Element Again." *Los Angeles Times,* June 21. https://www.latimes.com/entertainment/la-ca-yvonne-rainer21-2009jun21-story.html.

Kale, Shelly. 2015. "The 50th Anniversary of L.A.'s Watts Riots: Anna Halprin and the Studio Watts Workshop." *Experiments in Environment: The Halprin Workshops 1966–1971,* August 11. https://experiments.californiahistoricalsociety.org/the-50th-anniversary-of-l-a-s-watts-riots-anna-halprin-and-the-studio-watts-workshop.

Kaprow, Allan. 1993. "Happenings in the New York Scene (1961)." In *Essays on the Blurring of Art and Life.* University of California Press.

Kelsey, Karla. 2017. "Missing Contexts: The Pioneering Work of Halprin, Forti, and Rainer." *BOMB Magazine,* September 11. https://bombmagazine.org/articles/missing-contexts-the-pioneering-work-of-halprin-forti-and-rainer.

Kendall, Marisa. 2018. "Oakland's Creative Homeless Housing Solution Expands to Popular Local Hangout." *The Mercury News,* October 2.

https://www.mercurynews.com/2018/10/02/oaklands-creative-homeless-housing-solution-spreads-to-popular-local-hangout.

Klaus, Carl H. 1991. "Montaigne on His Essays: Toward a Poetics of the Self." *The Iowa Review* 21, no. 1: 1–23. https://www.jstor.org/stable/20153066.

Klaus, Carl H., and Ned Stuckey-French, eds. 2012. *Essayists on the Essay: Montaigne to Our Time.* University of Iowa Press.

Koch, Stephen. 1972. "Performance, a Conversation." *Art Forum,* December. https://www.artforum.com/features/performance-a-conversation-209908.

Kotz, Liz. 2014. "Simone Forti and Sound." In *Simone Forti: Thinking with the Body,* edited by Sabine Breitwieser. Translated by Nick Somers. Hirmer Publishers.

Kramer, Michael J. 2019. "The Mind Is a Muscle: Postmodern Dance and Intellectual History." *Society for U.S. Intellectual History,* June 30. https://s-usih.org/2019/06/the-mind-is-a-muscle-postmodern-dance-and-intellectual-history.

Krashen, Stephen D. 2009. *Principles and Practice in Second Language Acquisition.* Internet edition. http://www.sdkrashen.com/content/books/principles_and_practice.pdf.

Krauss, Rosalind E. 1977. *Passages in Modern Sculpture.* MIT Press.

"Kuchi-shōga." *TaikoSource.* https://www.taikosource.org/resources/taiko-basics#h.rfv5ikoudv4v.

Lambert-Beatty, Carrie. 2008. *Being Watched: Yvonne Rainer and the 1960s.* MIT Press.

Laramie, Joe. 1996. "Fourteen Years and Waiting: Pippin Ascends to Center Stage." *Prep News LX(21),* February.

LaRoche, Holly. 2020. "The Importance of Groove: Black Art As the Pillars of American Dance." *Dance Informa,* July 3. https://www.danceinforma.com/2020/07/03/the-importance-of-groove-black-art-as-the-pillars-of-american-dance.

Lim, Nancy. 2016. "MoMA Collects: Simone Forti's *Dance Constructions.*" *Inside/Out,* January 27. https://www.moma.org/explore/inside_out/2016/01/27/moma-collects-simone-fortis-dance-constructions.

Miller, Scott. 1995. "Inside *Pippin*: Background and Analysis." *New Line Theatre.* http://www.newlinetheatre.com/pippinchapter.html.

Morris, Terry. 2012. "Shootin' with Care: Safer Injection." Presentation by Terry Morris, Coordinator, The Speed Project, San Francisco AIDS Foundation. November. Personal communication.

Morse, Meredith. 2010. "Voice, Dance, Process, and the 'Predigital': Simone Forti and Yvonne Rainer in the Early 1960s." *VOICE: Vocal Aesthetics in Digital Arts and Media,* edited by Norie Neumark, Ross Gibson, and Theo van Leeuwen. MIT Press.

———. 2016. *Soft Is Fast: Simone Forti in the 1960s and After.* MIT Press.

Mullen, Harryette. 2002. *Sleeping with the Dictionary.* University of California Press.

Murphy, Cheryl G. 2015. "How Do Ballerinas Spin without Getting Dizzy?" *HuffPost*, October 28. https://www.huffpost.com/entry/how-do-ballerinas-spin-wi_b_8189718.

Museum of Modern Art. n.d. "Yvonne Rainer: *The Concept of Dust, or How Do You Look When There's Nothing Left to Move?*" https://www.moma.org/calendar/performance/1514.

Newton, Michael, and Emmalea Russo. 2016. *Eternal Apprentice*. DoubleCross Press.

Oregon Zoo. n.d. https://www.oregonzoo.org.

———. 2018. "Turtle Power: Baby Western Pond Turtles Arrive at Zoo." October 2. https://www.oregonzoo.org/news/2018/10/turtle-power-baby-western-pond-turtles-arrive-zoo.

Palmer, Michael. 2010. "The Recovery of Language." In *A Community Writing Itself: Conversations with Vanguard Writers of the Bay Area*, edited by Sarah Rosenthal. Dalkey Archive Press.

Perron, Wendy. 2017. "The Halprin-Forti-Rainer Postmodern Sweep." *Wendy Perron*, February 9. https://wendyperron.com/the-halprin-forti-rainer-sweep-of-postmodern-dance/.

———. 2021. "Simone Forti: BodyArtNature." *Wendy Perron*, March 22. https://wendyperron.com/simone-forti-bodyartnature/.

Pomeroy, Jordana. 2010. "Louise Bourgeois: A Legend." *National Museum of Women in the Arts*, June 4. https://nmwa.org/blog/louise-bourgeois-a-legend.

Pomeroy, Ross. 2013. "7 Facts You Didn't Know about Elephant Trunks." *RealClear Science*, October 15. https://www.realclearscience.com/blog/2013/10/the-most-amazing-appendage-in-the-world.html.

Powell, Kimberly. 2006. "Inside-Out and Outside-In: Participant Observation in Taiko Drumming." In *Innovations in Educational Ethnography: Theories, Methods, and Results*, edited by George Spindler and Lorie Hammond. Lawrence Erlbaum Associates.

Prendergast, John J. 2015 *In Touch: How to Tune In to the Inner Guidance of Your Body and Trust Yourself*. Sounds True.

Rainer, Yvonne. 1965. "*Trio A*, Yvonne Rainer." *MoMA Learning*. Archived at: https://web.archive.org/web/20230601175746/https://www.moma.org/learn/moma_learning/yvonne-rainer-trio-a-1978/.

———. 1966. "Hand Movie." Film, 8:00. Online excerpt hosted by Performa. https://vimeo.com/475658456.

———. 2006. *Feelings Are Facts: A Life*. MIT Press.

———. 2008. "A Manifesto Reconsidered." In *Manifesto Pamphlet*, edited by Nicola Lees. Bedford Press. https://d37zoqglehb907.cloudfront.net/uploads/2020/03/Manifesto-Pamphlet-1.pdf.

———. 2012. "Judson at 50: Yvonne Rainer." Interview by David Velasco. *Art Forum*, July 20. https://www.artforum.com/interviews/judson-at-50-yvonne-rainer-31348.

———. 2015a. "The Value of 'The Big Snooze' and Contingent Matters." *Triple Canopy*, August 27. https://www.canopycanopycanopy.com/contents/the-value-of-the-big-snooze.

———. 2015b. "Yvonne Rainer and Charles Aubin in Conversation." Interview by Charles Aubin. *Performa*, October. Original article no longer available online. Partial reprint at: https://conversations.e-flux.com/t/yvonne-rainer-and-charles-aubin-in-conversation/2739/1.

———. 2016. "Yvonne Rainer." Interview by In Terms of Performance, edited by Shannon Jackson and Paula Marincola. http://intermsofperformance.site/interviews/yvonne-rainer.

———. 2017. "Polymath Yvonne Rainer Discusses How She's Remained Radical for 50 Years with RoseLee Goldberg." Interview by RoseLee Goldberg, with text by Blake Abbie. *Document*, January 2. https://www.documentjournal.com/2017/01/yvonne-rainer.

Rhythmyk. 2009. "Question Everything: Kiai." *True Tall Taiko Tales*, September 1. http://truetalltaikotales.blogspot.com/2009/09/question-everything-kiai.html.

Rosenthal, Nan. 2004. "Marcel Duchamp (1887–1968)." *Metropolitan Museum of Art*, October. https://www.metmuseum.org/toah/hd/duch/hd_duch.htm.

Roy, Sanjoy. 2010. "Step-by-Step Guide to Dance: Yvonne Rainer." *The Guardian*, December 24. https://www.theguardian.com/stage/2010/dec/24/step-by-step-yvonne-rainer.

Ryan, Maura. 2009. "The Shimmy Shake Protest: Queer Femme Burlesque as Sex Positive Activism." In *Visible: A Femmethology, Volume One*, edited by Jennifer Clare Burke. Homofactus Press.

Scalapino, Leslie. 2010. "Messing Up Linear Time." In *A Community Writing Itself: Conversations with Vanguard Writers of the Bay Area*, edited by Sarah Rosenthal. Dalkey Archive Press.

Schlenzka, Jenny. 2016. "Simone Forti." *Flash Art*, November 2. https://flash---art.com/article/simone-forti.

Schulz, Kathryn. 2015. "Sight Unseen." *The New Yorker*, April 6. http://www.newyorker.com/magazine/2015/04/13/sight-unseen-critic-at-large-kathryn-schulz.

Schwartz, Stephen, and Roger O. Hirson. 1972. *Pippin*. Motown Records.

Shakespeare, William. 1911. *The Complete Works of William Shakespeare*. Edited by William George Clark and William Aldis Wright. Grosset & Dunlap.

Sharp, John. 2015. "What Yvonne Rainer Taught Me about Experimental Game Design." *Hey. I'm John.*, April 3. http://www.heyimjohn.com/what-yvonne-rainer-taught-me.

Storr, Robert. 2017. "Narcissism and Pleasure: An Interview with Yvonne Rainer." *The Paris Review*, November 17. https://www.theparisreview.org/blog/2017/11/17/narcissism-pleasure-interview-yvonne-rainer.

The Heckscher Museum of Art. 2014. "Exposed: Eadweard Muybridge and the Study of Motion." https://www.heckscher.org/exhibitions/exposed-eadweard-muybridge-and-the-study-of-motion.

The Museum of Modern Art. 2015a. "Yvonne Rainer discusses 'The Concept of Dust' with curator Ana Janevski." *YouTube*, September 21. https://www.youtube.com/watch?v=Sj4OysMPjio.

———. 2015b. "Yvonne Rainer, Live Performance: 'The Concept of Dust, or How do you look when....?' | MoMA LIVE." *YouTube*, June 13. https://www.youtube.com/watch?v=AAp9S4D27Vo.

University of Connecticut School of Fine Arts. n.d. "Puppet Arts Courses." https://drama.uconn.edu/programs/puppet-arts/puppet-arts-courses.

Walker Art Center. 2011. "Talking Dance: Yvonne Rainer and Sally Banes." *YouTube*, October 26. https://www.youtube.com/watch?v=cn6HtsbThKc.

Walsh, Jack, dir. 2016. *Feelings Are Facts: The Life of Yvonne Rainer.* Jack Walsh LLC.

Walz, Robin. 2008. *Modernism.* Pearson.

Waters, Flavie, Vivian Chiu, Amanda Atkinson, and Jan Dirk Blom. 2018. "Severe Sleep Deprivation Causes Hallucinations and a Gradual Progression toward Psychosis with Increasing Time Awake." *Frontiers in Psychiatry* 9, no. 303. DOI: 10.3389/fpsyt.2018.00303.

Wong, Deborah. 2000. "*Taiko* and the Asian/American Body: Drums, *Rising Sun*, and the Question of Gender." *the world of music* 42, no. 3: 67–78. https://www.jstor.org/stable/41692766.

Wood, Catherine. 2007. *Yvonne Rainer: The Mind Is a Muscle.* Afterall.

———. n.d. "Yvonne Rainer—Exhibition Text." *Raven Row.* http://ravenrow.com/texts/59/.

Young, Ralph. 2015. *Dissent: The History of an American Idea.* New York University Press.

Zdrojewski, Julia. 2014. "In the Margins: Dance Studies, Feminist Theories and the Public Performance of Identity." MA thesis, The College at Brockport, SUNY.

www.ingramcontent.com/pod-product-compliance
Lightning Source LLC
LaVergne TN
LVHW081259100826
845148LV00005B/920

9781685711887